Bush Theatre

HEART WALL

by Kit Withington

Heart Wall is a Bush Theatre production, co-commissioned with Oldham Coliseum. It premiered at the Bush Theatre, London, on 7 April 2026.

HEART WALL
by Kit Withington

Cast

Valentine	Aaron Anthony
Charlene	Olivia Forrest
Franky	Rowan Robinson
Linda	Sophie Stanton
Dez	Deka Walmsley

Creative Team

Director	Katie Greenall
Set & Costume Designer	Hazel Low
Lighting Designer	Simisola Majekodunmi
Sound Designer & Composer	Mwen
Movement Director	Mateus Daniel
Costume Supervisor	Esther Taylor
Casting Director	Jatinder Chera
Production Dramaturg	Ryan Hay
R&D Dramaturg	Ellie Fulcher
Dramatherapist	Wabriya King
Vocal Coach	Joel Trill
Makeup & SFX Artist	Katie Grist
Production Manager	Chloe Stally-Gibson
Company Stage Manager	Chloe Wilson
Assistant Stage Manager	Rhea Cosford
Stage Management Placement	Aino Teppo

For Bush Theatre

Lead Producer	Emma Halstead
Lead Dramaturg	Olivia Poglio-Nwabali
Original Dramaturg	Titilola Dawudu
Marketing Campaign Lead	Kelly Thurston
Technical Manager	Jamie Haigh

Special thanks to Conrad Lynch, Lynette Linton, Daniel Bailey, Mimi Findlay, Lauren Clancy, Nikita Karia, Sophie Cox, Philip Whitchurch, Lucy Black, Pedro Leandro, Alicia Forde and Jack Robertson.

CAST

Aaron Anthony | Valentine

Theatre includes: *A Christmas Carol, A Doll's House* (both Sheffield Crucible); *Cymbeline, Macbeth, Much Ado About Nothing* (all Shakespeare's Globe); *The Motive and the Cue* (National); *Yellowman* (Orange Tree); *Shakespeare in Love* (West End); *Twelfth Night, Billy Liar* (both Royal Exchange); *Lose Yourself* (Sherman); *Romeo and Juliet* (Insane Root); *A View from the Bridge, Macbeth* (both Tobacco Factory); *'Tis Unmanly Grief* (Theatre N16); *Human Emotional Process* (Chaskis/Arts Theatre).

Television includes: *The Blame; Emmerdale; Midsomer Murders; Father Brown; The Pact; The Other One; Shakespeare & Hathaway; Doctors; Outlaws; Witless; Holby City; Behind Her Eyes; Delicious.*

Short film includes: *I, You; Silent Phantom.*

Olivia Forrest | Charlene

Theatre includes: *Little Death* (Theatre503); *Much Ado About Nothing* (National); *Two Into One* (Mill at Sonning).

Television includes: *Falling.*

Rowan Robinson | Franky

Rowan studied at RADA, and was the winner of the Sir Alec Guinness Award in 2022.

Theatre includes: *A Taste of Honey* (Royal Exchange); *When We Are Married* (Donmar).

Television includes: *Brassic; A Knight of the Seven Kingdoms; Passenger; A Cruel Love: The Ruth Ellis Story.*

Film includes: *A Haunting in Venice.*

Sophie Stanton | Linda

Sophie is a fixture on national television, film and on the UK stage, and has made notable appearances in over forty of the biggest television shows of the last two decades. She has also appeared in numerous plays at the National, the Donmar, the Almeida – Diyan Zora's *Roots* being her fourth Almeida show – and for companies including the Royal Shakespeare Company and Paines Plough.

Theatre includes: *East is East* (National); *As You Like It, The Taming of the Shrew, The Fantastic Follies of Mrs Rich* (all RSC); *Ink* (Almeida); *The Tempest* (Donmar); *Henry IV* (Donmar & St Ann's Warehouse, NY).

Television includes: *EastEnders; King Gary; Endeavour IV; The Halcyon; My Mad Fat Diary; Gimme Gimme Gimme; Prime Suspect; A Touch of Frost; Ashes to Ashes; New Tricks; Where The Heart Is.*

Deka Walmsley | Dez

Deka is a British film, TV and stage actor.

Theatre includes: *Ghosts* (Lyric Hammersmith); *Roots/Look Back in Anger, Enemies* (all Almeida); *Fisherman's Friends: The Musical* (Hall for Cornwall); *A Midsummer Night's Dream, As You Like It, The Tempest* (all Shakespeare's Globe/tour); *An Enemy of the People, Wonderland* (both Nottingham Playhouse); *Macbeth, The Pitmen Painters* (both National/tour); *Secret Heart* (Royal Exchange); *Cyrano* (Bristol Old Vic); *Home Shetland* (National Theatre of Scotland); *Their Very Own and Golden City* (Royal Court); *Playing with Fire* (National); *Keepers of the Flame* (RSC); *Bones* (Hampstead); *Andorra, Stars in the Morning Sky* (both Northern Stage); *Billy Elliot, Cooking with Elvis, Blood Brothers* (all West End).

Television includes: *Forever Home; Truelove; Deceit; The Bastard Son & The Devil Himself; The Thief, His Wife and the Canoe; Vera; Three Girls; Our Friends in the North; Nature Boy; Ticket to Ride; Rebus; Waiters; Breeze Block; Grease Monkey; 55 Degrees North; Waking the Dead; Dirty War; Inspector George Gently.*

Film includes: *Blue Jean; A Banquet.*

CREATIVE TEAM

Kit Withington | Writer

Kit is a playwright from Manchester. She was a member of the Soho Theatre Writers' Lab in 2018, and her play *Scrap* was shortlisted for the Tony Craze Award. She was also part of the Emerging Writers' Group at the Bush in 2021, and has been part of both an Intro Group and a Long Form Group at the Royal Court.

In 2021 she wrote *Our Moon Under Water* for Edition 6 of the Royal Court's LIVING NEWSPAPER, and her play *As We Face the Sun* was produced by the Bush for their 18-25 Young Company in 2023. In 2025, her first radio drama *Nearly Light* was Highly Commended for Best Single Original Drama at BBC Audio Awards.

Katie Greenall | Director

Katie Greenall (she/they) is a director, theatre maker, and writer based in NE London/Manchester, specialising in new writing, solo autobiographical work, and youth/community projects. They are Associate Director (Creative Exchange) at the Royal Exchange Manchester, and previously Associate Director at the Bush Theatre, where she also led the Young Companies. Notable directing credits include *COMMUNION*, *As We Face the Sun* (Offie-nominated), *ANTHEM*, *Pass It On* and *Back Up!* (Bush) and *We All Know How This Ends* and *here, here, here* (Stratford East). They were also the Associate Director on *Barcelona* at the Duke of York's Theatre.

As a writer, Katie was part of the Roundhouse Poetry Collective and a Resident Artist (2018–19). She has been long-listed for the Channel 4 Screenwriting Course, alumni of the Soho Writers' Course, and was a finalist for the Popcorn Award in 2023. Her solo show *FATTY FAT FAT* won the VAULTS Origins Award (2019) and had a sold-out run at the Edinburgh Festival Fringe. Their current solo show *BLUBBER* explores body image through synchronised swimming and whales, and after a critically acclaimed run at Summerhall in 2024, tours nationally and internationally in 2026.

Hazel Low | Set & Costume Designer

Hazel is a performance designer and collaborator across theatre, live art and spatial design.

Theatre includes: *Playfight* (Paines Plough, Roundabout & UK tour); *The Glorious French Revolution* (New Diorama); *Blubber* (Summerhall); *The Legend of Ned Ludd* (Liverpool Everyman); *succession theme is my ringtone* (Rose); *Tiger* (Omnibus); *Bonfire* (Derby, Sheffield, Nonsuch); *As We Face the Sun, Pass It On* (both Bush); *Who Killed My Father* (Tron & Scottish tour – Co-Designer with Blythe Brett); *Splintered* (Soho); *Brilliant Jerks* (Southwark Playhouse); *Paradise Now!* (Bush – Co-Costume Designer and Design Associate); *I, Joan* (Shakespeare's Globe – Design Associate); *Bogeyman* (Pleasance Queendome); *The Magic Flute* (Royal College of Music – Co-Designer with Rosie Elnile); *Trainers* (Gate – Design Assistant).

Spatial design projects include: NDT Broadgate (Design Associate) and the Royal Court's pop up bar, Court in the Square, in 2021.

Mateus Daniel | Movement Director

Mateus is a movement director, choreographer and facilitator from South London. He has built a love and curiosity for telling stories physically that express themes of culture, change and transitions, and has used his experiences within dance and theatre to influence his current gothic lyrical style. His work can be seen on various leading UK stages, magazines and films and his personal projects thematically take on a melodramatic, gothic perspective. In addition, Mateus was a 2022 nominee for Best Choreographer or Movement Director for the Black British Theatre Awards.

As Movement Director: *Passion Fruit* (New Diorama); *Human Nurture* (Theatre Centre/tour); *Chicken Burger and Chips* (Brixton House); *The Boys are Kissing* (Theatre503); *Vardy v Rooney: The Wagatha Christie Trial* (Ambassador); *Our Eyes Look to God* (Festival d'Aix-en Provence); *What I Hear I Keep, I'll Burn the Ocean/For You* (Talawa); *As We Face The Sun, Communion* (both Bush); *TERRA XYZ* (Wonderland magazine); *TRIBE* (Young Vic); *Stranger Things: The First Shadow* (Phoenix), *No More Mr Nice Guy* (Broadway/Bristol Old Vic); *Vitamin D* (Soho); *Purgatory* (Donmar); *B*tch Boxer* (Watford Palace); *a practical guide on how to save the f***ing world when no one else is...* (Tara); *Spectacle of the Surreal* (V&A); *How to Win Against History* (Bristol Old Vic); *Safe Space* (Chichester).

Simisola Majekodunmi | Lighting Designer

Simisola trained at the Royal Academy of Dramatic Arts (RADA) with a degree in Lighting Design.

Theatre includes: *The Ballad of Hattie and James* (Kiln); *A Taste of Honey*, *Electric Rosary* (both Royal Exchange); *Metamorphosis* (Frantic Assembly, UK tour); *I, Daniel Blake* (Northern Stage & UK tour); *Choir Boy* (Bristol Old Vic); *Es & Flo* (Wales Millennium Centre); *Sound of the Underground*, *Is God Is*, *Living Newspaper* (all Royal Court); *Family Tree* (Belgrade & UK tour); *Treason: The Musical in Concert* (Theatre Royal Drury Lane); *J'OUVERT* (Theatre503/West End); *Starcrossed* (Wilton's Music Hall); *A Christmas Carol* (Shakespeare North); *Nine Night* (Leeds Playhouse); *Human Nurture* (Sheffield); *The Wiz* (Hope Mill).

Dance includes: *Dark with Excessive Bright* (Royal Opera House); *Traplord* (180 Studios); *The UK Drill Project* (Barbican); *Born to Exist* (Netherlands & UK tour); *AZARA – Just Another Day & Night* (The Place); *Puck's Shadow* (Watford Palace).

Mwen | Sound Designer & Composer

Mwen is a multifaceted artist, working as a theatre sound designer and composer, music producer, and live performing artist. Their creative practice blends the realms of music technology, electronic music, live sound, and performance.

Esther Taylor | Costume Supervisor

Esther is a fashion stylist working on commercial and editorial projects. She studied Textile for Fashion Design at Manchester School of Art and has worked for brands like Getty Images, Nike, John Lewis, Jack Wills and ASOS. She joined the world of costume for the first time for *Not Your Superwoman* at the Bush.

Jatinder Chera | Casting Director

For the Bush: *Heart Wall, Miss Myrtle's Garden, Lavender, Hyacinth, Violet, Yew, The Real Ones, A Playlist for the Revolution, Sleepova, The P Word*.

Other theatre includes: *The Waves* (Jermyn Street); *Marriage Material* (Lyric Hammersmith); *Scenes from a Repatriation*, *G* (Royal Court); *The Comeuppance* (Almeida); *The Flea, Samuel Takes a Break, Multiple Casualty Incident* (The Yard); *Sweat* (Royal Exchange).

Awards include: Olivier Award for Outstanding Achievement in an Affiliate Theatre, *Sleepova* and *The P Word*.

Ryan Hay | Production Dramaturg

Ryan is a Scottish writer, director and dramaturg based between Glasgow and Newcastle-upon-Tyne. As a writer, they have been commissioned by Eden Court, Ayr Gaiety, Northern Stage and Edinburgh International Book Festival, and were the 2020/21 Mayfesto Writer-in-Residence at Glasgow's Tron. In 2026 their play *Breathtaking Roads* opened at Glasgow's famous Play, Pie, Pint in a co-production with Stellar Quines.

Theatre includes: *My Name Is Rachel Corrie* (Alphabetti – Director), *BOOTCUT* (national tour – Director); *Little Miss Christmas* (Alphabetti & Southwark Playhouse – Director).

Ryan works extensively as a dramaturg, supporting the development of new work across scales and genres, and building producing models around ideas to meet audiences in traditional and found spaces. They are currently supporting projects at The Lowry, Pitlochry Festival Theatre and their own creative development company, wet arts ltd.

Ellie Fulcher | R&D Dramaturg

Ellie is a writer and dramaturg from South East London. She worked at the Royal Court Theatre from 2016 to 2024 as Literary and Participation Associate, contributing to main house productions and facilitating writer development work.

She currently leads Hackney Empire's writers' programme, as well as working on their Artist development programme. As a writer, Ellie won NBCUniversal and Soho Theatre's Overheard competition for her original audio comedy, *The Ballad of a Virgin Who Can't Drive*.

As a dramaturg, she has worked on plays including *Eat The Rich But Maybe Not Me Mates* by Jade Franks, *Why a Black Woman Will Never Be Prime Minister* by Zakiyyah Deen, and *Heart Wall* by Kit Withington at the Bush.

Titilola Dawudu | Original Dramaturg

Titilola Dawudu was previously Associate Dramaturg at the Bush, heading up the Literary department. She worked with the Artistic Director and Associate Artistic Director to commission and nurture new plays and ideas, working closely with writers, managing writing groups and the talent development pipeline.

Titilola was the dramaturg for an early iteration at Ovalhouse of Tyrell Williams's award-winning play *Red Pitch*. She dramaturgically supported some of the RSC's 37 Plays winners, most notably *Dreaming and Drowning* by Kwame Owusu.

Titilola co-created and edited *Hear Me Now: Audition Monologues for Actors of Colour* with Tamasha, published by Oberon Books. *Hear Me Now Volume Two* was published in August 2022 by Methuen Drama. As a writer, Titilola has written for Theatre Royal Arojah in Abuja, Nigeria, Theatre Peckham, Ovalhouse, Beyond Face and Soho Theatre.

Wabriya King | Dramatherapist

Wabriya is a qualified dramatherapist (Roehampton University), actress (Oxford School of Drama), creative facilitator and Reiki practitioner. She brings together her therapeutic and performance experience to support artists' wellbeing throughout rehearsals and production processes. From 2021–2025 she was Associate Dramatherapist at the Bush, working across all productions.

Her theatre work spans major UK venues including the National, Donmar, RSC, Almeida, Royal Court, Barbican, Young Vic, Old Vic, Soho Place, Lyric Hammersmith, and Stratford East. She currently provides support for West End shows *Wicked, Cabaret, Hamilton, Moulin Rouge* and *MJ The Musical*, as well as productions like *Prima Facie, The Boy Who Harnessed The Wind, Barcelona, Slave Play, A Strange Loop* and *Drive Your Plow Over the Bones of the Dead*.

Her screen work includes: *The Wolf Will Tear Your Immaculate Hands; The Changing Room; Empire of Light* and *Chevalier*.

Chloe Stally-Gibson | Production Manager

Chloe is a freelance production manager and former associate artist of Zoo Co Theatre Company and ChewBoy Productions.

Theatre includes: *Not Your Superwoman, Shifters* (also Duke of York's), *Tender, This Might Not Be It, Insane Asylum Seekers* (all Bush); *Punch, A Face In The Crowd* (both Young Vic); *Perfect Show for Rachel* (Barbican); *Playhouse Creatures* (JCTP); *Silence* (Tara).

Chloe Wilson | Company Stage Manager

Chloe is a stage manager and show caller. She studied at the Royal Central School of Speech and Drama.

As Company Stage Manager: *Potted Panto* (Apollo/The Core, Corby Cube); *Trainspotting Live* and *Oi Frog and Friends! Live* (UK tour); *An Evening with Sir Lenny Henry* and *August in England* (Bush); *Love Quirks* (The Other Palace); *Daniel's Husband* (Marylebone); *Afterglow* (Southwark Playhouse Borough).

As Stage Manager: *Club Nvrlnd, Flush, Brown Girls Do It Too* (Edinburgh Fringe); *Smithereens* (Brixton House).

As Deputy Stage Manager: *Red or Dead* (Liverpool's Royal Court); *La Tragedie de Carmen* (Buxton Opera House); *Spring Awakening* (Royal Central School of Speech and Drama).

As Assistant Stage Manager: *Windfall* (Southwark Playhouse); *L'Enfant Prodigue; Passion, Poison and Petrifaction* (Susie Sainsbury Theatre, Royal Academy of Music).

Rhea Cosford | Assistant Stage Manager

Rhea trained for an MA in Stage and Events Management at Royal Welsh College of Music and Drama.

As Assistant Stage Manager: *2:22, A Ghost Story* (Criterion); *Phantasmagoria* (Kali/Southwark Playhouse); *Who's Afraid of Virginia Woolf?* (Oxford Playhouse).

As Assistant Stage Manager (Book cover): *The Real Ones* (Bush); The Glass Menagerie (The Yard); *That Bastard, Puccini!* (RJG Productions, Park); *Three Little Pigs* (Unicorn).

Aino Teppo | Stage Management Placement

Aino is a prop maker and a stage manager in the making. She is currently in her second year at the Royal Academy of Dramatic Art, studying technical theatre and stage management, and working on *Heart Wall* by Kit Withington at the Bush.

Theatre includes: *After Miss Julie* (Park – Props Supervisor); *Bring It On!* (Beck – Assistant Stage Manager).

Bush Theatre

We make theatre for London. Now.

For over 50 years the Bush Theatre has been a world-famous home for new plays and an internationally renowned champion of playwrights.

Combining ambitious artistic programming with meaningful community engagement work and industry leading talent development schemes, the Bush Theatre champions and supports unheard voices to develop the artists and audiences of the future.

Since opening in 1972 the Bush has produced more than 500 ground-breaking premieres of new plays, developing an enviable reputation for its acclaimed productions nationally and internationally.

They have nurtured the careers of writers including James Graham, Lucy Kirkwood, Temi Wilkey, Jonathan Harvey and Jack Thorne. Recent successes include Tyrell Williams' Red Pitch, Benedict Lombe's Shifters, and Arinzé Kene's Misty. The Bush has won over 100 awards including the Olivier Award for Outstanding Achievement in Affliate Theatre for the past four years for Richard Gadd's Baby Reindeer, Igor Memic's Old Bridge, Waleed Akhtar's The P Word and Matilda Feyiṣayọ Ibini's Sleepova.

Located in the renovated old library on Uxbridge Road in the heart of Shepherd's Bush, the Bush Theatre continues to create a space where all communities can be part of its future and call the theatre home.

'The place to go for ground-breaking work as diverse as its audiences' EVENING STANDARD

bushtheatre.co.uk
@bushtheatre

THANK YOU

Our supporters make our work possible. Together, we're evolving the canon and creating a bolder, more diverse, and representative future for British theatre. We're so grateful to you all.

MAJOR DONORS
Charles Holloway OBE
Jim & Michelle Gibson
Georgia Oetker
Rajeev Philip
Cathy & Tim Score
Susie Simkins
Jack Thorne
Gianni & Michael Alen-Buckley

SHOOTING STARS
Jim & Michelle Gibson
Anthony Marraccino & Mariela Manso
Cathy & Tim Score
Susie Simkins

LONE STARS
Clyde Cooper
Adam Kenwright
Jim Marshall

HANDFUL OF STARS
Cyrus Benson
Charlie Bigham
Judy Bollinger
Richard & Sarah Clarke
Christopher delaMare
Sue Fletcher
Thea Guest
Kate Hamer Ltd.
Elizabeth Jack
Simon & Katherine Johnson
Garry & Lorna Lawrence
Phyllida Lloyd & Kate Pakenham
Vivienne Lukey
Sam & Jim Murgatroyd
Georgia Oetker
Mark & Anne Paterson
Miguel & Valeri Ramos Handal
Bhagat Sharma
Dame Emma Thompson
Joe Tinston & Amelia Knott

RISING STARS
Elizabeth Beebe
Martin Blackburn
David Brooks
Catharine Browne
Anthony Chantry
Lauren Clancy
Caroline Clasen
Susan Cuff
Matthew Cushen
Anne-Hélène and Rafaël Biosse Duplan
Austin Erwin
Kim Evans
Mimi Findlay
Jack Gordon
Hugh & Sarah Grootenhuis
Uzma Hasan
Lesley Hill & Russ Shaw
Davina & Malcolm Judelson
Joanna Kennedy
Mike Lewis
Lynette Linton
Tim & Deborah Maunder
Michael McCoy
Judy Mellor
Caro Millington
Rajiv Nathwani
Stephen Pidcock
James St. Ville KC
Jan Topham
Katja van Koten
Kit & Anthony van Tulleken
Angela Wachner

CORPORATE SPONSORS
Biznography
Casting Pictures Ltd.
Nick Hern Books
S&P Global
The Agency

TRUSTS & FOUNDATIONS
Backstage Trust
Buffini Chao Foundation
Christina Smith Foundation
Daisy Trust
Esmée Fairbairn Foundation
Garfield Weston Foundation
Garrick Charitable Trust
The Golsoncott Foundation
Hammersmith United Charities
The Headley Trust
Idlewild Trust
Jerwood Foundation
John Lyon's Charity
John Thaw Foundation
Martin Bowley Charitable Trust
Noël Coward Foundation
Royal Victorial Hall Foundation
The Thistle Trust

And all the donors who wish to remain anonymous.

If you are interested in finding out how to be involved, please visit **bushtheatre.co.uk/support-us** email **development@bushtheatre.co.uk** or call **020 8743 3584**.

HEART WALL

Kit Withington

Acknowledgements

Thank you to:

Everyone at the Bush. To Lynette Linton and Daniel Bailey. To the wider team and the new team.

To the talented cast and creatives. To Deka, Rowan, Sophie, Aaron and Liv.

To Katie Greenall, for committing to this story and joining me on the ride. Thank you so much.

To Titi Dawudu, for your early thoughts on the play. To Deirdre O'Halloran, for knowing exactly the right moment to get in touch. To Ellie Fulcher, for your strength and generosity. To Ryan Hay, for taking this on and having my back.

To Rupert Stonehill – the nicest Chelsea fan I've ever met.

To anyone who has ever been kind or, actually, even just normal when I have felt like an absolute nobody in a room full of people who knew how to finish a sentence. To anyone I was ever in a writing group with. To anyone who ever offered their time to read something I'd written, pushed me a bit or just told me to give it a go. To people like Stella, Ruth, Emily, Jeanie, Cat, Naomi and everyone at Ovalhouse those years ago. To Fiona Hamill and Katy Wyss. To Lucy Morrison and Jane Fallowfield. To Barbara Palcynzski. To everyone at Synergy Theatre Project, especially to Neil for reading the play and Esther and Jennie for endless support and understanding.

To a lot of good friends who I don't really deserve. To the ones who respected my efforts to not go out as much when working on this and to the ones who completely ignored it. What a laugh. To the ones spending small fortunes on trains to London from Manchester to see the play. Thank you for always reminding me who I am.

Special thanks to Dominic Cunniffe and Imogen Farrell for that time when you dropped everything, arrived immediately and got me to where I needed to be. I'll never forget it and I'll never forget the taxi driver who sobbed for his mum the whole way there. Thanks to him.

To Gemma.

To people who read the play or offered advice. To Katie, Farah, Kat, Tilly, Paige, Harry, Rosie, Holly, Sam, Faye, Abby, Nikhil, Phoebe, Hannah, Sophia and Grace. To Matt and Charlotte. To a living saint, Eve.

To my cousins, aunties, uncles. Thank you for teaching me the importance of spinning a good yarn. For showing up and for always knowing how to have a good time.

To Tina.

To my brothers, Patrick and Joe, you mean the world to me, actually.

To Our Vera, my mum. A masterclass in survival. Thank you for always being at the end of the phone. For talking complete shite to me even when you'd rather be watching something unmissable on Channel 5. In another life, I think you would have been a great writer. You are unbelievably special.

To my dad. There is absolutely everything to say and no way wide enough to say it. I love you and it's our tragedy that you are not here.

Finally, to the pubs, because at the end of it all, what else is there?

K. W.

'Her death was not my experience but her absence was.'

Louise Glück

Dedicated to my dad

Characters

FRANCES 'FRANKY' CARVER, *twenty-three*
DENNIS 'DEZ' CARVER, *sixties*
LINDA 'LIND' CARVER, *sixties*
CHARLENE 'CHARL' MARSHALL, *twenty-three*
VALENTINE 'VAL' HEENAN, *thirties*

Setting

A town in the north-west of England.

A pub, a living room, a moorland.

Notes

(–) suggests a trailing-off, an interruption or someone not knowing what to say.

Some words and phrases have been capitalised deliberately for emphasis.

Karaoke might be shortened versions of the songs.

This text went to press before the end of rehearsals and so may differ slightly from the play as performed.

Pre-show

*It is Friday night at The Sun Inn, known affectionately here as
'Sunny's'. This pub is a red mouth: wide open and soft with
carpet flooring. It is well worn but never scruffy. Wooden stools
with padded tops are tucked under tables. There is a dartboard
with plenty of holes around it. On the bar top, there are pickled
eggs in a jar. There are photographs, signs and trinkets that have
been there for a long time. There is a platform in front of
a curtain, a disco light that turns, and a telly, for karaoke.
A man in his thirties, VALENTINE, is carefully cleaning lipstick
off the edges of pint glasses. FRANKY, in her twenties, is sitting
next to a tote bag and drinking through a straw. She is waiting.
As the audience arrives, VALENTINE routinely opens a large
black ring binder, he tears empty slips and puts biros into a
basket, he checks a machine and finally, a microphone is placed.*

Disco lights. Karaoke.

*As soon as the audience is fully seated, lights change and
VALENTINE sings 'The Whole of the Moon' by The Waterboys.*

Scene One

FRANKY *is now in the living room of her family home. Her dad,
DEZ, is offstage. We can hear him crashing around in another
room. He has been disturbed.*

A beat.

FRANKY. Paul Scholes is dead.

   A bang.

   Dad?

   Paul Scholes has died.

DEZ. He's not?

FRANKY. He's gone.

DEZ. Have you checked online?

FRANKY *stares into a empty corner.*

FRANKY. His hutch.

DEZ. What?

FRANKY. His straw.

DEZ. Straw?

FRANKY. His bed.

DEZ. I thought you meant the bloody –

FRANKY. I meant The Bloody Rabbit.

DEZ. Honestly –

FRANKY. You forgot what I called My Bloody Rabbit.

DEZ. I haven't heard his name for a – have you still got your key?

FRANKY. My rabbit is dead.

DEZ. He's not dead.

He enters, flustered. He is struggling into a T-shirt, roughing up his hair.

He's missing.

When did you get back?

She's studying the empty corner as if a rabbit hutch might magically appear.

FRANKY. Before. Have you been out to look for him?

DEZ. Before what?

FRANKY. He'll be freezing cold. He's a house rabbit. He doesn't like the cold.

DEZ. This is a surprise. This. You. Here.

FRANKY. Are you pleased?

DEZ. Dead pleased. Will you come here.

A kiss on the head.

Did you ring?

FRANKY. No.

DEZ. I've not been on my phone.

FRANKY. I didn't ring.

DEZ. You know I would have picked you up from the station if I'd known. I would have met you on the corner by the Tesco Express.

You didn't ring first?

FRANKY. No I just –

DEZ. You just turned up.

FRANKY. Yeah.

DEZ. Off the train?

FRANKY. Yeah I did.

DEZ. Was it hectic?

FRANKY. Yeah it was –

DEZ. Was it absolutely rammed?

FRANKY. Yeah it was actually.

DEZ. You didn't have to sit on the floor did you?

FRANKY. No I had a seat. A table actually.

DEZ. Is Alfie not with you?

FRANKY. Alfie's got a tournament. He's been doing nothing but cold plunges for three weeks.

DEZ. He's committed.

FRANKY. He's irrational.

DEZ. That's why you've come home. Because Alfie's got a busy weekend, he's got a tournament and you'll be fed up.

FRANKY. I just wanted to see you.

>   Were you in the bath?

>   Your face it's a bit –

DEZ. I scrubbed it –

FRANKY. Blotchy. Is it a bit –

DEZ. – with the Bath Salts.

FRANKY. Bath Salts.

DEZ. Yeah. Bath Salts.

FRANKY. You're not meant to scrub your face with Bath Salts.

DEZ. Are you not?

FRANKY. No. You're meant to just pour them in. I was waiting for you at the pub. I thought something bad had happened.

DEZ. You were waiting at the pub.

FRANKY. You're always in the pub on a Friday night.

DEZ. Not tonight.

FRANKY. Normally you are.

DEZ. I fancied a bath. I was relaxing.

FRANKY. You were having a red-hot bath.

DEZ. It wasn't red-hot.

FRANKY. In the middle of July.

DEZ. Is it a crime is it that?

FRANKY. I waited two full hours and I thought –

DEZ. Two full hours.

FRANKY. I was going to jump right out from behind the bar. I had it all planned out.

DEZ. Did you?

FRANKY. I was going to scare you shitless.

DEZ. I've ruined it.

FRANKY. I thought you'd be pleased.

DEZ. I've ruined it by not being there.

   Beat.

FRANKY. My mum has told me about your red-hot baths.

DEZ. Has she?

FRANKY. She says you come out like a lobster.

DEZ. Is that what she says.

FRANKY. You have to have a little lie-down to come round
   again.

DEZ. Yeah well your mum prefers showers. Never trust anyone
   who doesn't like a bath, Frank.

FRANKY. Has she gone to get a takeaway?

DEZ. I've been trying a bit of – I think they call it – *Self-Care.*
   You should try it – *Self-Care.* Doing something for yourself.
   It might be one of the nicest things you can do for yourself,
   running a bath. That or putting a bit of Bonjela on an ulcer.
   They're both up there for me.

FRANKY. Has she gone to get a Raj Dan?

DEZ. I don't know –

FRANKY. I've not eaten all day. Could you send her a text?

   I don't want to spoil the surprise.

DEZ. No –

FRANKY. Just ask what she's getting, Dad. But don't mention
   a Biryani or a Prawn Bhuna or she'll know it's for me.

DEZ. I don't think she is –

FRANKY. Will you just ask what she's getting?

DEZ. She's not at the Raj Dan, Frank, she's at your nana's
   tonight.

FRANKY. On a Friday?

DEZ. There was a reason –

FRANKY. You weren't listening.

DEZ. Honestly, I might have switched off.

FRANKY. When she gets back we can walk to the pub.

DEZ. The Pub.

FRANKY. It's karaoke tonight.

DEZ. It's karaoke seven nights a week, Frank. A new thing
Valentine's trying. It's like being in Benidorm.

We didn't used to need karaoke in there.

We used to just have a sing-song. Someone would pipe up
and the rest of us would join in. We didn't have microphones
and backing tracks.

FRANKY. We can look for the rabbit on the way.

DEZ. You know, Frank, that rabbit – it was a kid's pet.

FRANKY. Yes me, I'm the kid!

DEZ. You're twenty-three. The point of getting the thing was so
you knew how it felt when something died.

FRANKY. He's not dead, he's missing!

DEZ. Well I've got a ready meal to eat.

FRANKY. We could eat that when we get back.

DEZ. Chicken Tikka Masala.

FRANKY. We can share it.

DEZ. Tesco's Finest.

I considered heating it up and having it in the bath but it's
a bit of a risk that. You don't want your Chicken Tikka
Masala getting mixed up with your bathwater.

FRANKY. You could text my mum and you could tell her to
hurry up back from my nana's house because you're itching
to get out of the house for a pint.

Where's your phone? Is it in your pocket?

I'll ring it. It might be down the settee.

She looks down the side of the settee for the phone.

Did you have it in the bath? Shall I get it?

I'll get it.

FRANKY *goes to leave.*

DEZ. I think she's staying actually.

FRANKY. Where?

DEZ. At Nana's. I think she's staying the night.

FRANKY. She never stays the night.

DEZ *flicks through records, he chooses something carefully, he takes the record out of the sleeve, places it on the record player.*

DEZ. There was something they wanted to do in the morning. An appointment. It might have been her hair or do you know what I think it might have been her toenails. To be honest it turns me off. Talk of your nana's toenails.

Have you ever seen your nana's toenails? Have you ever just caught sight of them, Frank? They're like little shovels on the end of each foot. You want to find yourself the nearest pin and stick it into each one of your eyes the second you've seen them.

FRANKY. Dad –

DEZ. She always has her shoes off. She won't mither with slippers.

FRANKY. Me and you could go to the pub just us two.

He fixes the needle. The record starts to play. It's 'In Dreams' by Roy Orbison.

DEZ. You used to dance to this. Whenever we put this on you'd dance to it.

He turns around the room, an arm opened out and a hand on his tummy.

FRANKY. Did I?

DEZ. You've not forgotten!

FRANKY. I can't remember.

DEZ. Outside in the garden. You used to send yourself dizzy.

DEZ *looks outside into the garden, listening to the song.*

FRANKY. We were never in the garden.

DEZ. What about those barbecues?

FRANKY. Barbecues.

DEZ. Lamb kebabs. Do you not remember my lamb kebabs?
Bit of mint, bit of garlic.

Yogurt sauce. You loved my yogurt sauce. Your mum would
do a Sangria.

FRANKY. Sangria?

DEZ. Red wine and Fanta. We've not done that for years.

FRANKY. I don't remember.

He stops dancing now, turns the music off.

DEZ. You never really come home.

FRANKY. It's expensive.

DEZ. Missed you that's all.

FRANKY. I thought I might go Over There while I'm back.

DEZ. Over where?

FRANKY. To the cemetery. I could take some flowers before
I go.

DEZ. How long you staying for, Frank?

FRANKY. The weekend. Are you okay? It's nice to see you.
It feels good to –

DEZ. Just the weekend?

FRANKY. Yeah. I wanted to ask you –

DEZ. Just till Sunday is it?

DEZ *puts his shoes on.*

FRANKY. Yeah. What are you doing?

DEZ. I thought you wanted to go to the pub.

Scene Two

*Same night. Background music is playing at Sunny's.
VALENTINE ducks in and out of the bar. He is jumping
between pouring drinks and keeping the bar running smoothly.
FRANKY is at the bar. DEZ follows in.*

DEZ. A man in the toilet just offered me a little line of cocaine.

FRANKY. You what?

DEZ. A bit of Chizz –

FRANKY. Sorry?

DEZ. A bit of Gak –

FRANKY. Yeah, Dad, we know what cocaine is.

    It doesn't really make it clearer if you use other words –

DEZ. He offered me some and then before I could answer, he
    sniffed a little mound of it off his knuckle.

    Straight up the nostril.

FRANKY. People in the toilets doing coke –

VALENTINE. I can hear you.

DEZ. How many years have I been coming in here and never
    have I ever been offered a bit of the stuff – never once have
    I been offered a bit of it –

VALENTINE. Yeah alright, Dez. I get it.

DEZ. I've created extra work. I have haven't I, Frank? He'll
    have to make a little sign now.

FRANKY. Are you doing those drinks, Val?

DEZ. He'll have to get his felt tips out.

VALENTINE. You're a pain in the arse –

DEZ. And you're a pain in my wallet. Have you put the prices
    up again?

VALENTINE. You say that every time you come in. He says
    that every time he comes in.

DEZ. Because every time I come in, it jumps up. Tell Eileen
    I want a word with her.

VALENTINE. Have you paid or –

FRANKY. Not yet.

DEZ. I'll tell her myself. Is she in?

FRANKY. I'd love to see Eileen.

VALENTINE. She's fast asleep.

DEZ. I'll go and make her a cup of tea.

VALENTINE. You'll disturb her.

> VALENTINE *takes the money, tries to hand the change to*
> DEZ. DEZ *holds a hand up to refuse it,* VALENTINE *tips*
> *the coins into a glass behind the bar.*

FRANKY. Alfie said it's brilliant sunshine in London.

VALENTINE. Is it fuck.

FRANKY. He said it is.

VALENTINE. What's he doing is he in a 'beer garden'?

FRANKY. I don't know if he is.

DEZ. We've got a beer garden here haven't we –

VALENTINE. Yeah except it's a car park attached to The Big
    Asda.

FRANKY. He said it's been cracking the flags all day.

VALENTINE. They lie about the weather in London all the
    time.

FRANKY. No they don't, course they don't.

VALENTINE. Capital city. They do it all the time.

DEZ. He's right, Frank, they do. They make it up.

FRANKY. You'll believe anything.

VALENTINE. I won't.

FRANKY. Have you ever had a Black Sambuca?

DEZ. No I don't like funny drinks.

FRANKY. Let's have a Black Sambuca.

VALENTINE. It makes your sick turn black.

FRANKY. Shall we have one?

DEZ. Are you right in the head?

FRANKY. We should celebrate really.

DEZ. Celebrate what?

FRANKY. Me. Coming home.

DEZ. You want to celebrate yourself.

FRANKY. I haven't seen you in almost a year.

DEZ. If it'll put a smile on your face.

VALENTINE *pours the shots, plonks them on the bar.*

VALENTINE. Two Black Sambucas.

DEZ. Three. If I'm having one, you're having one.

VALENTINE *pours another.*

FRANKY. To me being home.

DEZ. Christ Almighty.

They cheers, shoot the drinks, they taste terrible.

Jesus, that's absolutely awful.

FRANKY. I think that's nice.

DEZ. It's very –

FRANKY. What?

DEZ. Cloying. It's very cloying. Am I right or am I right?

FRANKY. Are you alright?

DEZ. It feels like I've burned a little hole in my throat –

I'm serious. Has it burned a little hole in the centre of my throat? Is it leaking? Is my throat leaking?

VALENTINE. You're so dramatic.

DEZ. It feels like there's been a little explosion in my
oesophagus.

He edges off. VALENTINE *shouts after him.*

VALENTINE. Shitbag you, Dennis.

FRANKY. Yeah well you're sweating. You've got little beads of
sweat running down your forehead.

VALENTINE *wipes it.*

My mum's at my nana's.

VALENTINE. Is she?

FRANKY. Did you not know? She's staying the night.

VALENTINE. No I didn't know.

FRANKY. It's different now you're in charge.

VALENTINE. Is it?

FRANKY. You look different now.

VALENTINE. Do you think this lot would let me get away with
looking different. I only have to get a new spot and they
want to know where it's come from.

FRANKY. Have you still got your other job?

VALENTINE. Every day until lunchtime.

FRANKY. And you're doing this as well.

VALENTINE. That's show business.

FRANKY. It would drive me mad –

VALENTINE. I like the contrast.

FRANKY. Flitting between the two.

VALENTINE. It keeps my mind busy. It's good for the brain,
I reckon.

FRANKY. And Eileen –

VALENTINE. Means I get to keep an eye on her.

FRANKY. She just stays upstairs sleeping.

VALENTINE. It confuses her coming downstairs.

FRANKY. She's forgotten who you are.

VALENTINE. She hasn't.

FRANKY. My mum said she's forgotten who you are.

VALENTINE. You know in four weeks, she'll be the oldest landlady in this country. They want to do a picture in the paper.

FRANKY. That's amazing.

VALENTINE. She wants to go back to Ireland. She mentions it every day. 'I want to go to Ireland to see my sisters.' She never forgets her sisters. It's not really possible not if she can't come downstairs but it's nice to have something to reach for sort of thing –

FRANKY. You should frame it. When they do her picture in the paper. You should put it up behind the bar.

Do you think my dad's alright?

VALENTINE. Does he seem alright?

FRANKY. Cos he's been in the toilet for quite a while. Do you think he's okay?

Beat.

What?

VALENTINE. What?

FRANKY. You want to say something.

VALENTINE. He was outside in the middle of the night.

FRANKY. In the middle of what night?

VALENTINE. In the middle of last night. He was cutting down the High Road, charging down the pavement in the pouring rain.

FRANKY. What were you doing awake in the middle of the night?

VALENTINE. I was cleaning up. It takes for ever.

FRANKY. I bet you're absolutely fucked going over to your
    telecoms job if you're cleaning up in the middle of the night.

VALENTINE. Yeah well, I'll sleep when I'm dead.

FRANKY. I think you've got too much on.

VALENTINE. I haven't.

FRANKY. You look tired. Do you feel it?

    DEZ *walks right back in.*

DEZ. There's a drip.

VALENTINE. What?

    VALENTINE *comes from around the bar. Just off, a little
    pool of water has gathered.* DEZ *and* VALENTINE *look at it.*

DEZ. Can you see that look. There's a drip coming from the
    ceiling.

VALENTINE. There is as well.

FRANKY. Were you being sick?

DEZ. I was rinsing my mouth out.

FRANKY. I thought you were being sick.

DEZ. It'll ruin the carpet that.

FRANKY. You smell a bit like sick.

DEZ. Summer rain. There's nothing like it.

    DEZ *places an empty glass to collect the drops.*

VALENTINE. It'll cost me a fortune.

DEZ. If water soaks into the carpet, the floor will start to smell.

VALENTINE. You said, Dez.

DEZ. A slipped slate on your roof I reckon.

FRANKY. It can drive someone mad a drip. We knew someone
    who had a drip coming from the pipe upstairs and it drove
    him so mad he ended up headbutting his own living-room
    wall. Do you remember?

DEZ. He needed stitches.

FRANKY. Can't you look at it, Dad?

DEZ. Me?

FRANKY. Yeah.

DEZ. I've just put a glass down. Did you not see me put a glass down?

VALENTINE. I'll have to call someone out.

DEZ. You know, Val, I think I can just about see the sky if I close one eye.

Scene Three

Sunday. Early. FRANKY *pulls on a string light as* DEZ *enters.*

DEZ. You scared the life out of me.

FRANKY. You woke me up.

DEZ. I didn't mean to.

FRANKY. Where've you been?

DEZ. Putting the bins out.

    DEZ *switches the telly on. The whole room is lit up blue.*

FRANKY. Putting the bins out in the middle of the night.

DEZ. The humpback whale.

FRANKY. You've seen this before.

DEZ. The first time I watched this I burst into tears.

    I don't mind telling you that.

FRANKY. It's only a whale.

    DEZ *turns right around in his seat.*

DEZ. *Only* a whale?

FRANKY. Mum's still at Nana's.

DEZ. She'll have her wiping her arse and all sorts knowing your nana.

FRANKY. Maybe I should go over and see her.

DEZ. Oh I like this bit Frank, where the whale cops off.

FRANKY. Cops off!

DEZ. Like a couple of kids down the boozer, Frank. You watch. Look he's gonna start singing in a minute. Brilliant singers these lot.

FRANKY. You were gone for ages.

He turns the telly up a bit.

DEZ. See him.

FRANKY. Yeah.

DEZ. He might sing this song for up to twenty minutes.

FRANKY. Your shoes are covered in mud.

DEZ. Fancies himself as a bit of a crooner, what do you reckon?

FRANKY. They're absolutely caked in it.

DEZ. Bit of a Frank Sinatra or a –

FRANKY *switches the telly off.*

I was enjoying that.

FRANKY. I saw you turn off at the end of our street.

DEZ. It turned into a little stroll that's all.

FRANKY. A little stroll at that time.

DEZ. A little stroll is good for you. It's sitting on your arse that will kill you.

Do you know I haven't been to see a doctor in thirty years.

I don't mither with doctors. Just look at me.

FRANKY. I think I will go over to my nana's.

DEZ. You'll be needing a lift to the station soon won't you?

FRANKY. Not yet.

DEZ. Not yet but soon.

FRANKY. I haven't even looked at the trains.

DEZ. You don't want to be getting yourself back late.

FRANKY. There's loads of trains. They run all day.

DEZ. You don't want to be getting back in the dark is all.

Sunday service, Frank. It slows things right down.

FRANKY. I've only been here five minutes and you're –

DEZ. It's flown by. I thought that.

FRANKY. Yeah it's –

DEZ. Have you sorted your stuff?

FRANKY. Not yet.

DEZ. You should sort it.

Pack your bag.

Get things ready.

It's awful when it's a rush.

FRANKY. I will.

DEZ. Go on then.

FRANKY. Can you just –

DEZ. Shape yourself, Franky. Bloody hell.

FRANKY. I can sense you getting –

DEZ. Getting what –

FRANKY. Getting wound up.

DEZ. I'm not wound up in the slightest.

FRANKY. No? Okay.

DEZ. I'm cool as a cucumber.

FRANKY. Are you?

DEZ. I'm just thinking of you and the dark and London and the
    Tube and the –

    LINDA *enters with a suitcase.*

LINDA. Franks –

DEZ. Bloody hell, Lind.

FRANKY. Hi Mum.

LINDA. I didn't know you were home.

    Is everything okay?

FRANKY. Everything's fine, Mum.

DEZ. You're back early aren't you?

    I didn't think you'd be back till much later.

    I thought your mum would have had you run ragged you see.

FRANKY. How is my nana?

LINDA. Your nana? She's. She's Your Nana –

DEZ. I bet she had you scrubbing the floor and all sorts.

LINDA. She's alright.

DEZ. Had you doing her a steak and chips I bet.

LINDA. She's fine.

DEZ. Well done. Cut the fat off. Salt, no vinegar.

LINDA. Dennis.

FRANKY. How was the spare bed?

LINDA. Same as usual.

FRANKY. The old fridge-freezer?

LINDA. Still buzzing.

DEZ. Fridge-freezer in the bedroom. It's not normal is it?

FRANKY. You'd be better on the settee.

DEZ. I've told her that.

 Haven't I said that, Lind?

 You'd be better on the settee.

LINDA. What about you coming back and not saying anything
 at all.

FRANKY. Did you bring something back?

LINDA. Back?

FRANKY. From Nana's.

LINDA. Oh no. I didn't bring anything back.

FRANKY. You took so much stuff.

 A whole case.

 Do you normally take a whole case?

DEZ. Indecisive. Aren't you, Lind? Aren't I always saying that?
 Indecisive.

 Do you want me to take your stuff up?

LINDA. No it's alright.

DEZ. I'll take it. Here.

LINDA. It's fine, Dennis.

DEZ. It's in the way to be honest.

LINDA. Yep. Fine. Okay. Take it. Go on.

DEZ. I'll take it and I'll put it by our bed.

LINDA. Right. Thank you.

 DEZ *exits with* LINDA*'s bag. A brief silence as he goes.*

FRANKY. You look nice.

LINDA. Do I?

FRANKY. Yeah you look really. Your skin. You look like
 you've had a fantastic sleep.

LINDA. I've not seen you in so long.

FRANKY. It's been over a year.

LINDA. It's never been so long has it. Let me look at you. Go on let me.

FRANKY. I am.

LINDA *hugs her.*

LINDA. It's good to see you.

FRANKY. Is it?

LINDA. Yeah. Are you okay?

FRANKY. I feel really good.

LINDA. I love it when you say that. Jesus, your dad still hasn't cut that grass. Do you know he's been saying he'll do it and he still hasn't.

FRANKY. He was in the bath when I got back. He was red raw.

LINDA. Was he?

FRANKY. Honestly he looked like he'd been scrubbed alive.

DEZ *walks back in.*

LINDA. How's Alfie's lovely mum and dad?

FRANKY. Yeah they're fine. They're good.

LINDA. Do they still take you out for nice meals?

FRANKY. Sometimes they do.

LINDA. What was that one you went to?

FRANKY. François'.

LINDA. That was it. François'. You had the confit duck.

DEZ. I bet they don't have soup of the day in François'.

LINDA. No, Dennis, of course they don't.

DEZ. I'm enjoying this.

LINDA. I can't believe I nearly missed you.

DEZ. You'd have been gutted, Lind. She would, she'd have been gutted.

FRANKY. You were rushing me off.

LINDA. What time's your train?

FRANKY. I can get any.

LINDA. You haven't booked it?

FRANKY. No cos I can get any.

DEZ. Till what time? That's what I want to know.

LINDA. They'll probably stop running soon.

DEZ. On a Sunday they will.

FRANKY. I can get any train within the next thirty days.

LINDA. Thirty days!

DEZ. And she complains about it being expensive.

FRANKY. Yeah cos I'm thinking. I'm thinking that actually –

DEZ. Complains about the timetables being to pot and –

LINDA. Dennis –

FRANKY. I might just stay.

Beat.

I feel like I've only just got here.

DEZ. You got here on Friday.

FRANKY. I've hardly seen my mum yet have I?

I've not even looked for my rabbit.

LINDA. Your rabbit.

FRANKY. I think he'll respond to my voice if I go out and call him.

LINDA. You won't be skiving work will you?

DEZ. It'll set you right back.

FRANKY. I've got holiday to take.

DEZ. It won't be much of a Holiday.

FRANKY. I can work from home.

DEZ. A Holiday in this weather.

FRANKY. Just for a few days.

LINDA. Well that'd be –

DEZ. Yeah that would.

LINDA. Great. Right then.

DEZ. You're all decided.

FRANKY. Yeah I think I am.

DEZ. You're staying.

FRANKY. Just for the week.

Scene Four

A girl in her twenties, wearing a silver puffa jacket zipped right up to her chin, is singing 'Freed from Desire' by Gala. This is CHARLENE *and she is bringing the house down.* FRANKY *is standing in front of her.* VALENTINE *is working behind the bar. The song finishes.*

CHARLENE. Frances Carver.

FRANKY. I hate it when you do that.

CHARLENE. What? When I do your full name?

FRANKY. Yeah.

CHARLENE. Okay, *Franks*. What are you doing here?

FRANKY. You scraped your name into my wardrobe once.

CHARLENE. That was thirteen years ago.

FRANKY. You scraped it into the wardrobe door with a pair of tweezers.

CHARLENE. I ruined a good pair of tweezers doing that.

FRANKY. *CHARLENE* in big curves in the wood.

CHARLENE. I got an inflamed follicle in my monobrow.

FRANKY. My mum said you'd be here. She said you'd be here at seven o'clock.

CHARLENE. You've changed your hair.

FRANKY. I used to let you put it into two plaits. You look exactly the same.

CHARLENE. It's a new coat this.

FRANKY. Are you not hot?

CHARLENE. I can't stand it when people say stuff like that.

If I was hot I'd take it off do you know what I mean?

FRANKY. You look a bit like you're hot.

CHARLENE. I haven't seen you in two years.

FRANKY. Do you want a drink?

CHARLENE. I want a red wine me.

FRANKY. You don't drink red wine.

CHARLENE. I do I drink it really often.

FRANKY. It gives me black teeth red wine.

CHARLENE. I don't mind having black teeth.

FRANKY. You don't mind having black teeth.

CHARLENE. It makes me look older.

FRANKY *takes the drinks.*

I reckon I look twenty-six when I've got black teeth.

CHARLENE *holds her glass of wine.*

Was it shit?

FRANKY. Was what shit?

CHARLENE. University.

FRANKY. I'm not at uni. I finished two years ago.

CHARLENE. Everyone's just back at their mum's.

FRANKY. I'm not. I'm in training.

CHARLENE. Everyone else.

FRANKY. I'm going to be an architect.

CHARLENE. Everyone else went away and now they're just
back at their mum's.

FRANKY. I live with my boyfriend in a flat. And anyway you're
still at your mum's. And to be honest you never even left.

CHARLENE. I'm just saying everyone said it was shit.

FRANKY. I work in an office.

CHARLENE. People who work in offices all just work from
home now. They might as well be anywhere.

FRANKY. You can see the whole city from the window.

CHARLENE. They reckon all these companies are sick to the
back teeth of paying rent with nobody going in. Money down
the drain they reckon.

FRANKY. I walk past The Palace sometimes. Have you ever
seen The Palace, Charl?

CHARLENE. What Palace?

FRANKY. Buckingham.

CHARLENE. Are you impressed by that?

FRANKY. No but it's a nice –

CHARLENE. The Royal Family. I didn't think you'd be
bothered.

FRANKY. The building itself is quite impressive.

CHARLENE. Do you wear a suit?

FRANKY. No it's very casual.

CHARLENE. I thought you'd have worn a suit. Pin-stripe.
Pencil skirt. A kitten heel maybe.

FRANKY. No it's not like that really.

CHARLENE. I thought it would have been.

FRANKY. It's not like that at all.

CHARLENE. That's London isn't it. They all go on nights out in woolly jumpers in London.

FRANKY. It's a big tall building where I work.

CHARLENE. Dancing to Techno in a knitted cardigan. Have you ever heard anything like it.

FRANKY. It's made completely out of glass. You might have seen it on the telly.

CHARLENE. I don't watch much telly.

FRANKY. You might not have realised.

CHARLENE. I only watch *Tipping Point.*

FRANKY. I'm the youngest in the office by four years.

CHARLENE. I work in the nursery now.

FRANKY. My mum and dad told me.

CHARLENE. I'm good at it. I'm patient.

FRANKY. I bet you are.

CHARLENE. I like having my own money to buy things.

FRANKY. Like that coat.

CHARLENE. I see your dad all the time.

FRANKY. He's never said.

CHARLENE. I seen him just last week.

FRANKY. You're not even drinking that.

CHARLENE. He goes past our window sometimes.

FRANKY. You haven't even had a sip.

CHARLENE. All times of night.

FRANKY. I paid for it.

CHARLENE. My mum's seen him on the Ring doorbell.

FRANKY. Does your mum still kiss that picture of Jesus on the cross every night?

CHARLENE. Every night and every morning. She prays for you. She prays for you and your mum and dad. She always has.

FRANKY. You can tell her that none of us believe in God.

CHARLENE. You're Catholic. You went to Our Lady's.

FRANKY. My dad says they're all raving lunatics.

CHARLENE *drinks a glug of wine. She needs it.*

I think it's really funny that neither of our parents have ever moved.

CHARLENE. I don't really think it is.

FRANKY. All those years in the same house.

CHARLENE. You've moved to a different city.

FRANKY. I always wanted to move house. I liked the idea of it. A big van coming for all our stuff. Eating fish and chips off the floor in a new home.

CHARLENE. You always wanted new things.

FRANKY. We used to say as soon as we were old enough, we'd buy our own flat. Open-plan. Big windows –

CHARLENE. And a brand-new kitchen.

I dreamt about you.

FRANKY. Did you?

CHARLENE. Nightmares sometimes.

FRANKY. You've always had nightmares.

CHARLENE. I don't mind them cos then it's quite nice when you wake up you're just in your bedroom underneath the covers.

FRANKY. Do you not want to move out ever?

CHARLENE. I like hearing them all through the walls.

Our Natalie's got a baby now. They live in the room next door. Do you want to see a picture?

She shows a photograph on her phone.

Bobby.

We say he's like a baby made of sausages. He's two. Can you still call him a baby?

FRANKY. He's proper lovely, Charl.

CHARLENE. We could sing if you want.

FRANKY. I don't want to sing.

CHARLENE. We could sing Little Mix.

FRANKY. I don't really like Little Mix.

CHARLENE. You used to really like Little Mix.

FRANKY. Not as much as you liked Little Mix.

CHARLENE. We danced to Little Mix at your eighteenth.

FRANKY. I don't feel like singing.

CHARLENE. You're funny you.

Beat.

FRANKY. I've still got it.

CHARLENE. What?

FRANKY. I think my bedroom is exactly the same as the last time you saw it.

CHARLENE. I thought it would be.

FRANKY. Single bed, picture in the frame hanging up on the wall and the same wardrobe with *CHARLENE* carved into the door.

CHARLENE. Do you know what, Frank, you aren't really that different. Behind your hair I can see your face and your –

FRANKY. You never came round to mine again after you did that did you.

CHARLENE. You remind me of your dad sometimes.

FRANKY. Do I?

CHARLENE. Yeah you do. You remind me of Dez.

CHARLENE *really looks at* FRANKY, *studies her for a second, a brief smile. She leaves.*

Scene Five

Later. FRANKY *walks into the living room where* DEZ *is standing.*

DEZ. I've been waiting for you look. I've been waiting, thinking where is she at all?

FRANKY. You're all on edge. Why are you all on edge?

DEZ. Look what I did I cut the grass. I bought a strimmer. I've been meaning to do it for absolutely ages and then there I was in the middle of Argos after work.

FRANKY. You've been to Argos.

DEZ. Did you know they have screens now in Argos? No catalogues any more. It only cost me thirty quid. It's a decent bit of kit. Have you seen it? It's like Old Trafford that grass.

FRANKY. You've never cut the grass before.

DEZ. You're mad with me for cutting the grass.

FRANKY. Why did we never move?

DEZ. We like it here.

FRANKY. I wish we'd moved. It's never been done. Is it even any different to when you first bought it?

DEZ. We painted the whole thing white once. There's no need to move when you can get yourself twelve tubs of Brilliant White, Frank.

FRANKY. You were awake in the night.

DEZ. Not all night.

FRANKY. You ran yourself a bath.

DEZ. What?

FRANKY. You ran yourself a bath in the middle of the night.

DEZ. I was hot. I was sweating cobs in the night. We haven't got the right duvets for the summer. I've told your mum we haven't got the right togs.

FRANKY. You could have washed your face in the sink, had a quick shower.

DEZ *moves away, ignores her.*

The wallpaper in the bathroom has started bubbling up underneath.

DEZ. Has it?

FRANKY. It smells a bit.

DEZ. Don't say that.

FRANKY. If I scratch my fingernail on it, I can see the yellow underneath.

DEZ. I'd leave it then me. Why would you scratch at it?

Scene Six

Friday night. A bar on the other side of town. LINDA sits at a table with a drink. She is wearing a lovely top. A going-out top. FRANKY arrives. She is wearing a jacket.

FRANKY. I like your top.

LINDA. Franky –

FRANKY *sits down on another chair.*

FRANKY. I like your top. Those straps –

LINDA. You've seen it before.

FRANKY. I haven't seen you wearing it since my eighteenth.

LINDA. Have you not?

FRANKY. I'd forgotten all about it.

LINDA. What are you doing here?

FRANKY. I fancied a drink. Shall we have a drink?

LINDA. I've got a drink.

FRANKY. You've nearly finished.

LINDA. It's a bit warm in here. Don't you think it's a bit warm.

FRANKY. I'm not that warm.

LINDA. It feels it.

FRANKY. You're all pink at the neck.

LINDA. We could go somewhere else.

FRANKY. There's a singer.

LINDA. Is there?

FRANKY. A tribute act.

LINDA. Straight out of Blackpool probably.

FRANKY. A Lionel Richie tribute act.

LINDA. Is he?

FRANKY. You love Lionel Richie.

LINDA. I like some of his solo bits.

FRANKY. Do you do this do you come in here on your own
    and have a drink?

LINDA. Sometimes I do.

FRANKY. I saw you at the bus station.

LINDA. Did you?

FRANKY. I saw you in that top and I thought I wonder where
    she's going in that top she wore for my eighteenth.

LINDA. Is that what you thought?

FRANKY. I watched you walk out of the exit. It was funny,
    you sort of walked through like you were swinging your
    shoulders.

LINDA. I don't think so.

FRANKY. I've never seen you swinging your shoulders before.
    It must be that top.

LINDA. Right well –

FRANKY. The way it hangs.

LINDA. Yeah.

FRANKY. And then after all that you were coming to the same place as me anyway. Isn't that mad?

LINDA. Yeah it is a bit.

FRANKY. Are you sure you don't want another one?

FRANKY *goes to the bar.* LINDA *checks her phone, sends a message.* FRANKY *takes her jacket off, folds it over her arm; she is wearing a short-cut top. She takes a drink over to the table.*

LINDA. Are you wearing a crop top?

FRANKY. Do you like it?

LINDA. It's too small.

FRANKY. Don't say that.

LINDA. It is. It looks ridiculous.

FRANKY. Everyone wears crop tops.

LINDA. It's not a crop top.

FRANKY. You just said it is.

LINDA *looks at the label at* FRANKY *'s neck.*

LINDA. It's age five to six.

FRANKY. It doesn't matter what it says on the label if you like it.

LINDA. It's from Tammy Girl.

FRANKY. I found it at the bottom of my wardrobe.

LINDA. You've washed it.

FRANKY. Can you tell?

I like the colour.

LINDA. It looks stupid.

FRANKY. I think it looks nice.

LINDA. Take it off.

FRANKY. In here.

LINDA. Yes.

FRANKY. I've got nothing underneath.

LINDA. Take it off and put your jacket on.

FRANKY. I don't want to.

LINDA. It looks stupid and silly and –

FRANKY. What?

LINDA. It's hard to look at you.

FRANKY. Why?

    Beat.

LINDA. I think you should go home and get changed.

    FRANKY *takes a sip of her drink.*

FRANKY. Your hair's gone lighter.

LINDA. Has it.

FRANKY. Your hair's gone lighter. You've have it done.

LINDA. I haven't.

FRANKY. You've got freckles.

LINDA. I've always got freckles.

FRANKY. I like your freckles.

LINDA. Do you?

FRANKY. I mean it.

LINDA. Thank you.

FRANKY. I've got your freckles.

LINDA. Yeah you have.

FRANKY. And when I see your freckles I think about my
freckles and the fact that when you're gone, when you've
died, I'll still have your freckles won't I.

LINDA. Why don't we go up the road.

FRANKY. I like it in here. I like the wallpaper. It's a lovely
    pattern.

LINDA. I'm really warm.

FRANKY. I think it'd look nice in our house.

LINDA. When that singer starts we won't hear ourselves think.

FRANKY. We can just watch.

LINDA. Right well I'm too hot!

FRANKY. Is he going to be here in a minute do you think?

LINDA. You followed me.

FRANKY. I saw a man on my way in who I've seen before.

LINDA. I think we should go actually.

FRANKY. I saw him and I remembered his face from your work.

LINDA. I think we should just go home.

FRANKY. I wanted to see who he was.

LINDA. We could walk back.

FRANKY. And then I realised I met him once and he gave me
    a two-pound coin.

LINDA. We could walk back and have a conversation.

FRANKY. Have you sent a text and cancelled? Told him to wait
    a bit longer? Meet you somewhere else?

LINDA. I'd like you to go home and take that top off and put it
    back where you found it.

FRANKY. I'll take it off.

LINDA. Good.

FRANKY. When I get home I'll take it off.

LINDA. Thank you.

FRANKY. And I'll run the scissors through it. I'll cut it into
    a hundred pieces and I'll put it back where I found it.

LINDA. You will not.

FRANKY. I want to.

LINDA. You can't.

FRANKY. I came home and I realised that there's so many things in my bedroom that don't belong to me.

LINDA. You don't live there any more.

FRANKY. I think I'll get rid of it.

LINDA. You haven't been home in a year.

FRANKY. Alfie says it's not good for you so much clutter. He says you need to clear your stuff to clear your mind sort of thing.

LINDA. It's not clutter.

FRANKY. Well what is it?

LINDA. You know what it is.

FRANKY. A shrine.

LINDA. It's not a shrine.

FRANKY. That's what it feels like.

LINDA. Don't be so –

FRANKY. One time you told me you don't like me.

LINDA. I don't think I did –

FRANKY. I love you I just don't like you. That's what you said.

LINDA. That's just a thing people say.

FRANKY. I don't know anyone who says it.

LINDA. I could drag some of the things up you've said to me over the years.

FRANKY. I think about it all the time.

LINDA. We could be here until next week if I did that.

FRANKY. Have you met him in here before?

I realised when I'm not here you could be meeting him whenever you want.

What do you do? Do you go round to his? Or is it just tribute acts? Is that your thing?

I think I'll tell him, my dad. About seeing you here. About you sitting here in your nicest top.

I think he deserves to know.

Are you laughing?

LINDA. Do you think your dad doesn't know?

Is that what you think?

That Dennis knows absolutely nothing at all.

Scene Seven

At Sunny's. CHARLENE and FRANKY sit either side of a table. They have the karaoke ring binder opened out in front of them. They are taking photographs of themselves on FRANKY's phone.

VALENTINE is behind the bar. There is a bucket now collecting the drips of water from the ceiling.

CHARLENE. Have you heard them having sex?

FRANKY. No I don't think so.

CHARLENE. You don't think so.

They stop posing, look at the picture.

FRANKY. No I haven't.

CHARLENE. That's a really nice one of me.

FRANKY. Yeah it is.

FRANKY places her phone down on the table.

CHARLENE. I hear mine all the time.

FRANKY. I'd absolutely hate that.

CHARLENE. I can hear them through the walls. It doesn't
    bother me at all. It's very healthy.

FRANKY. I don't like the idea of it that's all.

CHARLENE. Well they probably don't like the idea of you and
    your boyfriend going at it either.

FRANKY. They love Alfie.

CHARLENE. You've never said his name before.

FRANKY. Have I not?

CHARLENE. Alfie. Like Lily Allen's brother.

FRANKY. Alfie cos his dad's called Alan and his mum's called
    Fiona. So they stuck them together, actually.

CHARLENE. And if they were chocolate I reckon they'd eat
    themselves.

FRANKY. They're very interesting people.

VALENTINE. Interesting?

FRANKY. They're into taxidermy.

CHARLENE. Taxi-what?

FRANKY. Stuffing animals. You have to remove the skin and
    they put all sorts of chemicals into the body to keep it from
    rotting. Then you have to sew the skin onto something like
    a bit of foam or whatever.

CHARLENE. I was going out with a boy once who used
    a spoon to butter his toast. I thought that was interesting.

FRANKY. They have the family dog, stuffed and sitting there
    on the landing at his mum and dad's house. She's called
    Pesto.

VALENTINE. That's honestly fucked in the head.

FRANKY. She's a German Shepherd.

CHARLENE. He's got a German Shepherd called Pesto stuffed and sitting on his landing at his mum and dad's house.

FRANKY. It's a mark of respect.

CHARLENE. Our spaniel, Kevin, is just buried in a hole at the bottom of our garden.

FRANKY. In China they're forever speaking to the dead.

CHARLENE. Natalie thinks she can speak to the dead.

VALENTINE. How has she worked that one out.

CHARLENE. Cos we went to a see a clairvoyant and the clairvoyant looked her right in the eyes and dead serious she went 'I think you have the gift.'

FRANKY. What did you and Natalie go to a clairvoyant for?

CHARLENE. She asked me to go with her.

FRANKY. In some places like in Indonesia they keep the dead with them at the table and that. Dress them up, sit them up straight and bring them a bit of food or whatever. We learnt that in a lecture.

CHARLENE. The heart wants what the heart wants, Frank. That's what my mum says.

Buzzing. It's FRANKY*'s phone, she ignores it.*

Your phone is ringing.

FRANKY. I know.

CHARLENE. Answer it then.

FRANKY. I'll call them back.

Phone beeps, she turns it over.

CHARLENE. Is it work?

FRANKY. No it's not work.

CHARLENE. Is it Alfie?

You can answer it. I don't mind.

FRANKY. I don't want to answer it.

CHARLENE. I seen you with him once when you came back.

FRANKY. It's not Alfie.

CHARLENE. He has very straight teeth that's what I thought.

FRANKY. Do you want a packet of crisps?

FRANKY *goes up to the bar.*

Can we have some crisps?

VALENTINE. You can help yourself if you want.

CHARLENE. Like very naturally straight. Not like he's been
    to Turkey but like he's just been born with very naturally
    straight teeth. Has he had a brace ever or –

FRANKY. Do you still like Smoky Bacon?

CHARLENE. I prefer Pickled Onion.

The phone starts ringing again.

Your phone.

FRANKY. He's not got Pickled Onion. Have you got Pickled
    Onion?

VALENTINE. No. Your phone is ringing.

FRANKY. I think I'll have plain.

CHARLENE. Should I answer?

FRANKY. God you've got them all mixed up here. Nothing is
    in its right place. There used to be boxes for each flavour.

VALENTINE. Does it matter?

FRANKY. You haven't fixed the roof.

VALENTINE. They quoted me two grand.

CHARLENE. Franky!?

FRANKY. What will you do will you just leave it?

CHARLENE. Your fucking phone is fucking ringing.

FRANKY. He's got Worcestershire Sauce. Will you have Worcestershire Sauce?

CHARLENE *picks the phone up from the table. The phone rings out.*

CHARLENE. Hello, it's Charlene.

FRANKY. What the fuck are you doing?

FRANKY *comes out from the bar, takes the phone out of* CHARLENE*'s hand and puts it in her pocket.*

Are you stupid?

CHARLENE. I was joking. I was winding you up.

FRANKY. I don't find things like that funny.

CHARLENE. It rang off.

You're upset.

FRANKY. I'm not.

CHARLENE. I can always tell when you're upset.

Pause.

You've been here for nearly four weeks.

It'll be August soon.

FRANKY. I know what date it is, Charl.

CHARLENE. It'll be August soon and you'll have been here over a month.

FRANKY. I know.

CHARLENE. It's like you've moved back.

FRANKY. I haven't.

CHARLENE. Isn't Alfie bothered?

FRANKY. I've told him I won't be back until I've found Paul Scholes.

CHARLENE. Your rabbit.

FRANKY. My rabbit is missing.

VALENTINE. Your rabbit is missing?

FRANKY. I can't go back until I've found it.

VALENTINE. How long has it been missing for?

FRANKY. Since I've been back.

VALENTINE. You've been back for ages.

FRANKY. I left some Rib 'N' Saucy Nik Naks on the back step.

VALENTINE. What will you do if you don't find him?

FRANKY. He always liked Rib 'N' Saucy Nik Naks.

VALENTINE. Will you just stay?

Pause.

CHARLENE. You never asked me to come and stay with you.

FRANKY. Right well –

CHARLENE. You never asked. Not once. I thought you would.
  I thought you'd ask me to come and stay.

FRANKY. I've never had much room to be honest.

CHARLENE. I'd have slept on the floor. I'll sleep anywhere.
  People have always said that about me.

FRANKY. Well it's quite hard to just put aside a weekend.

CHARLENE. Is it?

FRANKY. Yeah it is.

CHARLENE. It doesn't sound very hard.

FRANKY. Once you start building a life for yourself it is.

CHARLENE. Is that what you've done? Built yourself a life. Is
  that what it feels like?

FRANKY. Yeah.

CHARLENE. The first time you ever stayed at my house you
  said you never wanted to leave. You said you liked the noise.

FRANKY. I didn't. You and your sisters fighting over the
  Variety Pack. It did my head in.

CHARLENE. I wet the bed once.

FRANKY. Yeah well you were only little. People do.

CHARLENE. You told people.

FRANKY. I told one person.

CHARLENE. I've been thinking about it.

FRANKY. What are you bringing that up for?

CHARLENE. My mum said he's not a full shilling your dad. She said you're the same. She said you've always been the same.

FRANKY *squashes the packet of crisps in her hands, throws it.*

Fucking hell –

VALENTINE. Frankyyyy!

FRANKY. What.

VALENTINE. You're up next.

FRANKY. Skip to the next person please, Val.

The backing track starts for 'Black Magic' by Little Mix.

VALENTINE. I'm afraid it's already started.

FRANKY *walks to the stage and sings, a bit reluctantly at first. Maybe she gets into it eventually. The song is a surprise to* CHARLENE. CHARLENE *and* VALENTINE *watch for a bit.* FRANKY *continues singing throughout the next conversation.*

She picked this for you.

CHARLENE. She has eighteen missed calls.

VALENTINE. So.

CHARLENE. Why is she still here?

VALENTINE. She wants to find her rabbit.

CHARLENE. She hasn't been bothered about that rabbit in four years.

VALENTINE. I told her to.

CHARLENE. To What?

VALENTINE. Dez knocking on my door in the middle of the night.

CHARLENE. When.

VALENTINE. Asking if he can talk to Eileen.

CHARLENE. You told her to come back.

VALENTINE. Asking if he can come up and talk to her in the middle of the night.

CHARLENE. Now she won't leave.

Scene Eight

In the living room. DEZ has been in the bath. He pulls his T-shirt up to his neck so that he can look at his back in a mirror. We can see that he has large red marks on his skin. He needs to sort of hug himself to see it properly. LINDA enters.

LINDA. Your back –

DEZ *flinches, covering himself again with his T-shirt.*

DEZ. Fucking hell, Linda.

LINDA. It's all marked.

DEZ. Creeping up on me like that.

LINDA. It's red raw.

DEZ. I thought you were out.

LINDA. Your skin is peeling. Show me.

She goes to lift up his T-shirt. He pulls away.

You've scalded yourself, Dennis.

DEZ. Can you not?

LINDA. It's only me, for God's sake.

DEZ. Only you?

LINDA. I could show you. If you want. I could hold up a mirror and show you.

DEZ. Oh you'd love that wouldn't you?

LINDA. I'll get you some antiseptic.

DEZ. Have a good laugh.

LINDA. It needs something or it will blister.

She finds a tube of antiseptic.

DEZ. I think it might be a rash. New washing powder or –

LINDA. I haven't bought new washing powder. Did you fall asleep in the bath?

DEZ. No.

LINDA. Did you drift off or leave the water running or –

DEZ. I don't know if I did.

LINDA. Are you in any pain?

DEZ. It's Friday. Don't you have somewhere to be?

LINDA. Let me see you.

DEZ. Cos I was thinking of watching the telly. I've got something to watch.

LINDA. Always the bloody telly.

He switches it on, flicks to something. It's a documentary.

DEZ. I love this programme. Every seven years they film this group of people. Have you seen it? Every seven years you see how they've changed, their ideas about things, There's a little lad on there from Skipton. He wanted to learn about the moon when he was seven.

'Give me the child until he is seven and I'll show you the man.' That's what it says, Lind, in the credits. This programme.

Honestly. Seeing someone's life laid out like that.

LINDA. Dennis!

DEZ. You should watch it.

LINDA. Stand up.

He doesn't.

Well go to a bloody hospital and let someone else do it then.

DEZ. What?

LINDA. You won't. You won't ever do that.

I know everything about you. You forget that I know everything about you.

DEZ. Shouldn't you be out tonight?

You probably have a meal booked. Should go and get yourself ready.

LINDA. Do you not want something else ever, Dennis?

DEZ. Have you finished?

LINDA. No.

DEZ. Go on, you best get going, Lind. At least this will be something to talk about.

Something to discuss over a bit of grilled fish.

LINDA. I've wanted to sleep with other men for years. But I haven't not until –

DEZ. Where is it tonight? One of them places in town with the white tablecloths? We'd have never gone to a place like that.

LINDA. We'd never go anywhere if it was down to you. You've ignored me for a long time.

Ignored what I've wanted. In a marriage, Dez. You're supposed to have a life together. That's what it's supposed to be. I've dreamed of another person sitting next to me and asking me what I think about something. I've dreamed of another person just looking me right in the eye.

He goes back to watching the telly.

DEZ. He was on the B team in football. Stephen.

LINDA. Okay Dennis.

DEZ. Just so you know.

He went to my school.

LINDA. I want a new life.

DEZ. Is that what it is?

LINDA. I do I want a whole new life.

DEZ. You want to leave.

LINDA. What would you do?

DEZ. I know you want to leave.

LINDA. What would you do if I left?

DEZ. You can't leave.

LINDA. What would you do. If I just did.

You'd just leave it wouldn't you.

Let your own skin fall off in your T-shirt.

DEZ stands up. LINDA lifts the bottom of his T-shirt, studies the marks on on his skin. She takes the tube of antiseptic, squeezes some onto her hands, rubs them together. DEZ lifts up his shirt.

Scene Nine

The Sun. VALENTINE *is holding something small and soft in his hand. It is wrapped inside a tea towel.*

FRANKY. It's not mine.

VALENTINE. It's a rabbit.

FRANKY. It's not mine. Mine's ginger.

VALENTINE. Is it not?

FRANKY. Yeah. Paul Scholes. Mine's orange.

That's more… Phillip Schofield.

VALENTINE. It's bald.

FRANKY. Okay then that's more… Pep Guardiola.

VALENTINE. I need to get rid of it.

FRANKY. What will you do with it?

VALENTINE. I'll put it back in the car park.

FRANKY. Put it by the tree.

VALENTINE. Yeah.

VALENTINE *holds it right out in front of him. He takes it outside again.*

FRANKY. Your roof is still leaking.

VALENTINE. Yeah, well, the rain hasn't stopped.

Have you spoken to your dad yet?

FRANKY. What about?

VALENTINE. You'll get the sack from that job.

FRANKY. It's shit anyway.

Do you know how people speak to you on the phone.

VALENTINE. You're working towards something. Do you know how many people would like to be working towards something?

FRANKY. You told me to come back.

VALENTINE. I didn't tell you –

FRANKY. You phoned me.

VALENTINE. I suggested.

FRANKY. You made me feel guilty.

VALENTINE. You know when I was little I wanted to be just like your dad.

FRANKY. No you didn't.

VALENTINE. I swear I did. I lived with my nana and grandad. Your dad was always full of beans. He would throw me on his shoulders or kick a football up into the sky like it was gonna disappear. I thought he was amazing.

FRANKY. People at uni hated their parents. Made me quite embarrassed that I liked mine.

VALENTINE. I don't think that's embarrassing.

Beat.

I had a dream the other night that I killed Eileen with a pillow.

Held it tight in the palm of my hand until I killed her with it.

Till her breath just stopped.

You weren't expecting me to say that.

FRANKY. You want to kill your nana.

VALENTINE. It was only a dream.

FRANKY. You'd get sent to prison.

VALENTINE. When I woke up I thought I'll close the bar, I'll pick her up in both arms and I'll take her on a plane to see her sisters.

FRANKY. Centre of midfield for Manchester United.

That's what you wanted to be when you were growing up. You wanted to be a footballer.

VALENTINE. Yeah when I was about twelve.

FRANKY. It doesn't bother you that you're –

VALENTINE. That I'm not a Premier League footballer? No it doesn't bother me.

FRANKY. They've got money coming out of their eyeballs.

VALENTINE. Do you know how many people would like to run a pub?

FRANKY. It's what you want.

VALENTINE. Yeah it is.

FRANKY. I don't know. I don't know if I want anything at all sometimes.

VALENTINE. You don't get it. I wake up in the morning and I don't worry at all about the day ahead. You can't understand that. That it's enough.

FRANKY. Do you not want a girlfriend ever?

VALENTINE. I have had –

FRANKY. Kimberley.

VALENTINE. Yeah.

FRANKY. You brought Kimberley back to the pub one time and it went totally silent.

VALENTINE. That was a baptism of fire.

FRANKY. I walked in on you kissing round the back of the bar, near the door where the cellar is. I was on my roller skates and I just stood there, held on to the side and watched. Your nan caught me staring.

VALENTINE. You little pervert.

FRANKY. I was only nine.

VALENTINE. You little Peeping Tom.

FRANKY. I was interested. The way you licked her neck.

VALENTINE. I've got to finish this.

FRANKY. I'd never seen anything like that before.

VALENTINE. There's all this still needs sorting.

FRANKY. One time I phoned you in the middle of the night and you picked me up from Birdcage in town.

VALENTINE. Yeah you were sick on my new trainers.

FRANKY. I was fifteen.

VALENTINE. I'd saved my wages to get them trainers. They were limited edition.

FRANKY. You let me hide in your living room until I sobered up. You made me soup and soft toast.

VALENTINE. On a tray. Like Eileen did.

FRANKY. You never told my mum and dad.

VALENTINE. You asked me not to.

FRANKY. They would have killed me.

VALENTINE. First rule of working behind the bar. If someone tells you something, you keep it exactly where they want you to keep it. To yourself.

FRANKY. Will you kiss me?

VALENTINE. No, Franky, I won't.

FRANKY. What if I told you that I actually wanted you to.

VALENTINE. I'd tell you that you're bored.

FRANKY. You wouldn't just do it.

VALENTINE. No I wouldn't.

FRANKY. If I kissed you, you wouldn't kiss me back.

VALENTINE. I wouldn't no.

FRANKY. You wouldn't lick my neck like you did Kimberley's?

VALENTINE. No I wouldn't.

FRANKY. You'd throw it away –

VALENTINE. Yeah.

FRANKY. Would you?

VALENTINE. I'd tell you to go back to London. To stop playing whatever games you're playing and stop running away from whatever you're running away from. And I'd tell you that I need to finish this delivery.

Scene Ten

DEZ *and* CHARLENE *are cutting past The Sun late at night.*

DEZ. I thought I could feel someone's eyes in the back of my
    head.

CHARLENE. I see you all the time.

DEZ. Shouldn't really be out at this time.

CHARLENE. I was at a nightclub and I started feeling really
    sick.

DEZ. Shouldn't really be out on your own.

CHARLENE. You are. You've not even got a coat. I said that to
    Franky. I said, he's never even got a coat.

DEZ. I used to do this walk when she was a baby.

CHARLENE. I saw where you came from.

DEZ. They like the movement babies.

CHARLENE. I know all about babies.

DEZ. Sends them off. Sometimes. Stops them crying.

CHARLENE. You made me cry once.

DEZ. Were you watching me?

CHARLENE. You held on to my shoulder and you shouted
    at me so much you left a bit of spit running down my face.
    Do you remember?

DEZ. You carved your name into our wardrobe.

CHARLENE. I was only ten.

DEZ. You carved it into the door in big letters.

CHARLENE. We used to do it in school.

DEZ. I couldn't get it off.

CHARLENE. Our names written on everything.

DEZ. You ruined the wood.

CHARLENE. You scared me.

DEZ. I didn't mean to scare you.

CHARLENE. Why are you out in the middle of the night?

DEZ. I can't sleep ever.

CHARLENE. Can you not?

DEZ. Makes me feel queasy. The trying.

CHARLENE. I used to pull my eyelashes out in my sleep. Have you ever done that before?

DEZ. That sounds painful. Why did you do that?

CHARLENE. I used to wet the bed sometimes.

DEZ. Why have you told me that?

CHARLENE. I never really understood it before –

DEZ. Understood what?

CHARLENE. Why you lost your temper like that. We're all hiding bits of ourselves aren't we? The bits we're not proud of. I can see that now.

Scene Eleven

FRANKY *is sitting in Sunny's.* LINDA *enters with carrier bags.*

LINDA. I found this in the British Heart Foundation.

FRANKY. At least it's going to a good cause.

LINDA. I had to buy it back. It cost me nearly fifty quid.

FRANKY. It'll go back in my room then?

LINDA. It's personal. It's not stuff anyone would want.

FRANKY. None of it's been touched for years. It's not been unfolded or washed or –

LINDA. So you thought you would just give it away?

FRANKY. I was surprised they took it to be honest. It's gone quite musty.

LINDA. I don't like the idea of other people with those things. It makes me feel funny.

FRANKY. Do you and Dad still eat your tea together?

LINDA. Sometimes.

FRANKY. Not always.

LINDA. No.

FRANKY. Do you still sleep with him?

LINDA. You should leave I think.

FRANKY. I'm not ready to.

LINDA. You've been here for weeks.

FRANKY. I think I can look after him.

LINDA. You can't.

FRANKY. I think I can help him.

LINDA. He doesn't need someone to cut up his spaghetti.

FRANKY. He needs someone to love him.

LINDA. I do –

FRANKY. You're fucking someone else.

LINDA. Can you not say fucking –

You're unhappy.

I can tell. I can always tell.

FRANKY. Why did you buy it back?

LINDA. Because it's mine.

FRANKY. What will you do with it?

LINDA. I'm going to put it back where it was.

FRANKY. You can take all of these things and put them in your boyfriend's house.

LINDA. He's not my boyfriend, Franky.

FRANKY. What is he?

LINDA. He's just a person who makes me feel good about myself.

FRANKY. My dad doesn't?

LINDA. No he doesn't. Not any more.

FRANKY. You could leave him.

LINDA. I can't just leave him, Franky.

FRANKY. I think that's kinder.

LINDA. I can't just fucking fucking fucking leave him.

FRANKY. You make him unhappy.

LINDA. You don't know anything about it.

FRANKY. I shouldn't have left.

LINDA. I'm glad that you don't.

FRANKY. He hasn't always been like this.

LINDA. No but he's never been easy. He's –

FRANKY. He's my dad.

LINDA. I'm glad actually. I am. That you don't understand.

FRANKY. If I move back in –

LINDA. Is that what you want?

FRANKY *puts on the Roy Orbison song.*

What are you doing?

FRANKY. He said when I was little we used to dance to this –

LINDA. Roy Orbison.

FRANKY. Yeah.

LINDA. You didn't dance to it. He used to play it and you'd go to sleep.

FRANKY. He said I danced to it.

LINDA. No you never danced to it. It used to send you off to
sleep.

LINDA *turns it off.*

FRANKY. Do you think I'm selfish?

LINDA. We can all be –

FRANKY. Do you think I'm a bitch?

LINDA. No I don't think that at all.

FRANKY. Do you think I'm a totally spoiled-brat selfish bitch?

LINDA. You're not.

I feel like that sometimes.

I don't think you are.

You should go back I think. I'll help you book a train.

FRANKY. I don't need help.

LINDA. Is it money? They're expensive. I know that they're
expensive.

FRANKY. I can't, not yet.

LINDA. You can't stay here.

FRANKY. Why can't I?

LINDA. You have a whole life. What about Alfie and your flat
and your job. You've not been there in a really long time.

FRANKY. What if it's not what I want.

LINDA. It's your life. It's what you've chosen.

FRANKY. Is that it? You just choose something and that's it.

LINDA. You must always listen to it, Franky.

FRANKY. Listen to what?

LINDA. That feeling you get in your belly. That *thing* you feel
when it's telling you to do something.

FRANKY. Is that what you're doing?

LINDA. I don't know.

FRANKY. Loads of people aren't that happy in marriages, Mum. Loads of them look shit.

LINDA. I'll never not love your dad, Franky.

FRANKY. But you've grown apart.

LINDA. Yeah.

FRANKY. And that's how you live?

LINDA. Yeah it is.

I want to get home from work and enjoy the evening. I want to make a plan for two months' time. I don't want to wait around for something to happen.

FRANKY. I'm sorry about the clothes. I wanted to make space in my room. Do you blame me?

LINDA. You know you won't remember this but when you were little you used to cling to me. It was quite hard actually. You wouldn't bloody go to anyone else.

FRANKY. Not even Dad?

LINDA. You liked to be just here. On my shoulder so you could see out. You used to pull on my earrings when I was talking to someone else. You pulled on this left one so hard once, the earring cut right through the lobe.

It doesn't just go away that stuff. It doesn't just mean nothing.

LINDA *picks up the carrier bags, about to leave.*

FRANKY. I don't have a thing.

LINDA. You will.

FRANKY. What if I don't ever have a thing?

LINDA. Course you will.

Beat.

LINDA *makes her way over to the stage, she takes the microphone and sings 'Brass in Pocket' by The Pretenders. She sheds something here, lets some of herself go a little bit.*

Scene Twelve

FRANKY *in Sunny's.* CHARLENE *enters. Beat.*

FRANKY. You're missing *Tipping Point.*

CHARLENE. You've let your ticket expire.

FRANKY. I've been looking for my rabbit.

CHARLENE. You're still looking?

FRANKY. The internet says to look underneath parked cars.

    Pause.

CHARLENE. It's my birthday today.

FRANKY. Charl, I'm sorry. I forgot.

CHARLENE. I thought you might have done.

FRANKY. I'm sorry I –

CHARLENE. There's a rave at Steppers later. Twelve different DJs. It's on till the morning.

FRANKY. I hate Techno.

CHARLENE. You hate other people's birthdays.

FRANKY. I don't.

CHARLENE. You always have.

FRANKY. You've made that up.

CHARLENE. Your seventh birthday party.

FRANKY. The Wacky Warehouse.

CHARLENE. You invited the whole class. Hardly anyone ever invited the whole class because it was a class of thirty-two, but you invited the whole class.

    You ruined it for everyone else.

FRANKY. I didn't.

CHARLENE. Nobody wanted to carry on playing because you were so upset.

FRANKY. I don't think I was.

CHARLENE. You hate other people's birthdays because you hate your own.

FRANKY. I'm sorry that I forgot your birthday, Charl –

CHARLENE. You're not the only one the world turns for, Franky. It turns for the rest of us as well.

FRANKY. I'll go to Steppers with you tonight if you really want.

CHARLENE. I wasn't inviting you.

FRANKY. If it means that much to you. I will.

CHARLENE. I'm not dragging you round Steppers with a face like thunder. I'm going with my sisters.

Beat.

FRANKY. Are you?

CHARLENE. Yeah.

FRANKY. Good.

CHARLENE. Your rabbit is in my garden.

FRANKY. What.

CHARLENE. He's been in my garden for months.

FRANKY. No he hasn't.

CHARLENE. Your dad gave Paul Scholes to Bobby.

FRANKY. I don't believe you.

CHARLENE. Natalie took him round to yours for his tea. Your dad made them a shepherd's pie.

FRANKY. No he didn't.

CHARLENE. Bobby asked if he could hold the rabbit. He held him on his knee and he loved him. He wouldn't stop loving him. So your dad just said keep him. Dez brought his hutch round and put it in our back garden.

FRANKY. He's a house rabbit. He shouldn't be outside in the garden.

CHARLENE. Your dad came round a couple of weeks ago asking for him back.

FRANKY. My dad came round to your house –

CHARLENE. Our Natalie said no. She said no, Bobby's too attached. He goes outside every morning and feeds him lettuce through the mesh wire.

FRANKY. Why have you told me?

CHARLENE. You can leave now can't you. You don't have to stay.

You're the same as your dad.

FRANKY. You've never liked my dad.

CHARLENE. Cut from the same cloth.

You let the world lay heavy on you both of you.

FRANKY. Yeah well my dad's been through a lot so –

CHARLENE. Do you think everyone else hasn't?

Everyone knows it's cos he blames himself. Everyone knows it's because he always has. Yeah, well so does your mum but she doesn't walk around like the world owes her something.

FRANKY. What have they got to blame themselves for?

CHARLENE. Why don't you just fucking ask.

Scene Thirteen

It is midday on the twenty-first of August. DEZ and LINDA are in the cemetery. LINDA separates a bunch of flowers and cuts the stems.

DEZ. Have you done what you needed to do?

LINDA. I just want to clean the stone, Dennis.

DEZ. Do you want this cloth?

LINDA. Yeah and that –

DEZ *passes her a cloth and a bottle of water.*

DEZ. Do you remember, Lind, after it happened and we went to see the doctor –

LINDA. Why?

DEZ. Do you remember?

LINDA. Why are you talking about that?

DEZ. Dunno I just thought of it.

LINDA. Course I remember.

She empties the bottle of water over the grave and lets it run.

There's all this bird muck look.

DEZ. They sit in that tree that's why.

LINDA. It annoys me. It's all stuck.

LINDA *gets a bit frustrated with it.*

DEZ. Here give it here.

DEZ *takes the cloth off her. They stand looking at it, the grave, taking it in for a while. After a bit…*

You've missed some of the birdshite, Lind.

LINDA. I've used the last of the water.

She passes back the empty water bottle.

DEZ. Where did you go on your holiday?

Beat.

Was there a beach?

Was it sunny?

A balcony in the sun.

I've imagined you on a balcony in the sun.

LINDA. You want to know.

DEZ. Yeah I do, I want to know.

LINDA. It was a city break actually.

DEZ. A city break.

LINDA. We went to Málaga.

DEZ. I imagined that you went to the beach.

LINDA. There is a beach.

DEZ. You said a city break.

LINDA. Yeah but there's a –

DEZ. We've never stayed in Málaga. We've flown to Málaga but we've never stayed in Málaga.

LINDA. Loads of little bars and –

DEZ. Is there?

LINDA. Yeah.

DEZ. Did you enjoy it?

LINDA. Yeah.

DEZ. Was it hot?

LINDA. It wasn't too hot. It was –

DEZ. It was just right?

LINDA. Yeah it was.

DEZ. You enjoyed it.

LINDA. Do you remember our holiday in Greece?

DEZ. –

LINDA. You washed my hair with a bottle of water from the shop. We danced on the rooftop until it dried didn't we?

I always liked being in different places with you, Dez. Your mind shifted. You thought differently. I've always said it's the light. It's the light in a different place that makes you feel something. Every city has a different light. I've always said that.

They look at the grave, a moment of reflection. LINDA *tries to find* DEZ*'s hand.*

DEZ. It was our last holiday without any children.

> *There is a brief moment of touch. It is difficult.*

> You never cried after.

> *DEZ breaks away from her. He can't.*

LINDA. I know.

DEZ. You never cried. I used to chew the duvet like a dog so you couldn't hear me but you. You never cried.

LINDA. I couldn't.

> *Beat.*

> I'm going to go and stay with Stephen for a bit.

DEZ. Are you?

LINDA. Yeah I am.

DEZ. You're going to move in with him.

LINDA. I'm just going to stay there for a few days.

DEZ. You hate sharing the bed.

LINDA. You're not on your own.

DEZ. You hate sharing *our* bed.

LINDA. I want to go and stay with him for a bit.

DEZ. It's like I'm ill isn't it.

> You're going for respite. One in, one out.

> She comes, you go. You leave, she stays.

LINDA. I'm just going there for a bit, Dez.

DEZ. I won't leave that house.

> Do you understand?

> I won't leave it.

> *DEZ takes another cloth from his pocket. He starts polishing the grave.*

> Here. Can you help me with this?

LINDA. I didn't ever expect you to ever get over it, Dennis, it's just that I thought we might find a life beyond it. That's all.

DEZ. Is that enough do you think?

LINDA *has left.* DEZ *continues polishing the stone.*

Scene Fourteen

Same day. The living room is lit up blue. FRANKY is watching the sea life programme. She is holding a framed picture. The picture inside the frame has been drawn by a small child. There are three large heads with long legs springing out of them. 'Mummy, Daddy, Me.' DEZ enters.

FRANKY. Did you know that her heart is the size of a small car?

DEZ. What's that?

FRANKY. The Humpback Whale.

DEZ. You've moved it.

FRANKY. What?

DEZ. You've moved that picture.

FRANKY. It was on my bedroom wall.

DEZ. I know where it was. I hung it up.

There'll be a mark.

FRANKY. I thought it would be nice to have it down here.

DEZ. There'll be a shadow from the dust.

FRANKY. A family picture.

DEZ. It's a *drawing*.

FRANKY. Long legs coming out of big heads… it's always scared me. The way it hangs over my bedroom. Why did you bother framing it?

DEZ. Some parents get rid of everything their kid brings home from nursery. We kept every single thing. Every birthday card. Every certificate.

FRANKY. I know it's bursting out of every drawer.

DEZ. You know you've been really quite messy since you came back.

FRANKY. I don't think I have.

DEZ. You have, you've been leaving things out. Cups, plates, knives and forks. It's like you turn into a child again when you come back.

FRANKY. You think I'm lazy.

DEZ. I think you're careless actually.

FRANKY. I annoy you, I can tell. I can always tell when I annoy you.

DEZ. You're like a baby that doesn't know how to use their legs yet.

FRANKY. You wish I didn't come back.

DEZ. Clumps of hair left in the bath, crumbs of toast in the butter.

And you know you're meant to put the lid back on the milk.

Cos you know that milk turns to cheese if you leave it on the side like that.

FRANKY. You want me to leave.

DEZ. You're not very good at taking criticism to be honest. You never have been.

FRANKY. You want me to leave so you can just stew like you were stewing before.

DEZ. You think I need looking after but at least I know how to put the milk away.

FRANKY. I think I'll go actually.

DEZ. Go where.

FRANKY. Home.

DEZ. Home. Makes me laugh when you say that.

FRANKY. Where's Mum?

DEZ. She's gone.

FRANKY. Did you upset her?

DEZ. –

FRANKY. I know what day it is today.

DEZ. –

FRANKY. I've been thinking about it all day.

DEZ. Yes well –

FRANKY. You're always like this. Do you know that?

DEZ. What?

FRANKY. Every year on this day you're like this.

DEZ. –

FRANKY. There's an argument.

DEZ. I don't think there is.

FRANKY. You make me feel like I'm in the way, like I shouldn't
be here.

DEZ. Maybe you shouldn't.

    Beat.

FRANKY. You look smaller you know. In this house. I've been
thinking that loads. How you fill a lot less of it now. The way
you stand.

    I thought it as soon as I saw you.

    It's a horrible feeling. Coming home and seeing you get
older and older.

    Beat.

    You gave away my rabbit.

DEZ. I tried to get it back.

FRANKY. You let me look for it but you gave it away. You gave it to Bobby.

I didn't know you still saw Natalie.

DEZ. I've known Natalie for thirty years.

FRANKY. You gave my rabbit to her son.

DEZ. He asked if he could see it and then he asked if he could hold it and I let him hold it and he just kept cuddling it.

FRANKY. I'll get my things.

All this over a stupid fucking –

DEZ. Drawing. Give it to me.

FRANKY. No.

DEZ *tries to take the frame out of* FRANKY*'s hands.*

Get off me.

DEZ. Seriously, Franky –

He tries to prise it from her. It's messy. A bit embarrassing. She doesn't let go.

FRANKY. You're hurting me.

DEZ. You fucking –

FRANKY *pulls away.*

FRANKY. My thumb.

FRANKY *releases the frame, it falls and cracks. A sheet of glass shatters onto the floor.*

DEZ. It's broken.

DEZ *is on all-fours now.*

FRANKY. You'll cut yourself. Stop it.

He doesn't stop. He is collecting the shards of glass, gathering them.

Look at you.

You're mad.

DEZ. We only ever wanted one child. Did you know that. We never really thought we could afford to have more than one.

Just saying – you know – if she hadn't died, you would never have been born.

FRANKY. It's like you've waited my whole life to tell me that.

DEZ. It wouldn't really have been possible.

Do you know what the chances are of any of us ever even being born at all is?

One in four hundred trillion. I looked it up.

He fiddles with the picture frame which is bent at the edges now.

You can't get your head round that can you? One in four hundred trillion.

It's hard to isn't it.

Sort of thing that can keep you awake all night.

DEZ *continues to fish through the broken glass.*

FRANKY. Stop it.

DEZ. It wasn't yours.

FRANKY. Stop it. Stop it –

DEZ. It wasn't yours to smash.

FRANKY reaches for the drawing which has fallen loose. The piece of paper is old, flimsy, a bit faded. She turns it over, holds it up to the light, the crayon markings are clearer now. She puts it down beside DEZ. He leaves.

Scene Fifteen

Sunny's. CHARLENE is watching the telly. VALENTINE places glasses back onto a shelf.

CHARLENE. There really is something about Ben Shephard.

VALENTINE. Do you think so?

CHARLENE. I reckon Ben Shephard keeps his side of the wardrobe absolutely immaculate.

DEZ *enters.*

VALENTINE. Alright, Dez.

CHARLENE. Oh look she's won a mystery prize.

VALENTINE. Do you want a drink?

DEZ. I thought you'd gone.

VALENTINE. You're shaking.

CHARLENE. Are you hungry? What about a pickled egg?

DEZ. I don't want a pickled egg.

CHARLENE You might need to eat.

DEZ. I don't need to eat, thank you.

CHARLENE. I know what day it is today.

DEZ. Do yer?

CHARLENE. It's the twenty-first of the month.

We lit a candle in our house this morning. We always do.

VALENTINE. I'll make you a drink. What will you have?

DEZ. You've not been here for ages.

VALENTINE. I got back today.

DEZ. I thought you'd packed up left, jacked it in, the lot.

VALENTINE. No it wasn't that.

DEZ. I thought you'd given it up.

VALENTINE. It was just a holiday.

DEZ. I was thinking all sorts.

CHARLENE. Where did you go?

DEZ. You never fixed the slate on the roof.

VALENTINE. No not yet. I will.

DEZ. Will you?

VALENTINE. Yeah.

DEZ. There's a bird's nest up there.

VALENTINE. I know.

DEZ. There's a bird's nest in the roof of the pub –

VALENTINE. I know, Dez –

DEZ. You've seen it?

VALENTINE. Yeah.

DEZ. Cos you can see it from the street outside.

VALENTINE. Yeah I've seen it.

DEZ. People will stop coming to the pub if they don't think it's
    being looked after.

VALENTINE. I'm back now.

DEZ. I've seen it happen plenty of times.

VALENTINE. I'll call someone to fix it.

DEZ. It's been weeks.

VALENTINE. I've been busy.

DEZ. Busy.

VALENTINE. Yeah.

DEZ. We're all busy, Val.

VALENTINE. I've been in Ireland.

DEZ. Have you.

VALENTINE. I've been in Ireland and I'm back now.

CHARLENE. I've never been to Ireland.

DEZ. It's unprofessional.

VALENTINE. Unprofessional?

DEZ. There'll be nothing left of this place if you aren't careful. Have you seen the state of the carpet. It's damp. I told you that the floor will start to smell. Water dripping through –

CHARLENE. Your hand is bleeding.

We hear an answer on Tipping Point. *There the sound of the audience clapping. Something snaps inside DEZ.*

DEZ. Can you turn that fuckin thing off.

CHARLENE is shocked and looks at him. Maybe this is the first time she's heard him lose his temper since the time when she was younger. A beat.

CHARLENE. There's blood going right down your arm.

DEZ. It's nothing.

VALENTINE. It's not nothing.

DEZ. I can't feel it.

VALENTINE. Have you hit something?

DEZ. No I've not hit something. It's nothing.

He tries wiping it. VALENTINE rummages for something, finds a box behind the bar.

VALENTINE. Let me look at it for you.

DEZ. Doesn't need looking it.

VALENTINE. Just give me your hand, Dez.

He pulls an alcohol wipe out of a packet.

DEZ. Oh look you've got a first-aid kit.

VALENTINE. Here.

DEZ moves into the light of the bar.

DEZ. Is that what you were doing in Ireland? Were you getting a certificate?

He looks to CHARLENE for a laugh here. VALENTINE takes DEZ's hand, rubs it with the wipe. It kills.

It's just a little bit of –

Argh you fucking cunt.

VALENTINE. Keep still.

DEZ. Get off me.

DEZ *moves away.*

VALENTINE. I haven't finished.

DEZ. I said it was nothing. Just leave it.

VALENTINE. You're trembling.

DEZ. I'm not scared of you.

VALENTINE. Let me clean you up.

DEZ. Hit me.

VALENTINE. What?

DEZ. I want you to hit me in the face.

VALENTINE. I'm not gonna do that.

DEZ. In fact I'm asking you to hit me.

VALENTINE. Calm down, Dez.

DEZ. Have you ever punched anyone in the face before, Val?
    I bet you haven't. I bet you've never thrown a punch.

VALENTINE. –

DEZ. Go on smash your fist into my face if you want. I'll let
    you.

VALENTINE. I don't want to.

DEZ. I'm telling you to.

VALENTINE. I'm not going to.

DEZ. Charlene?

CHARLENE. What?

DEZ. Will you hit me?

CHARLENE. Val?

DEZ. I bet you've always wanted to hit me, Charlene.

CHARLENE. I haven't.

VALENTINE. Fucking hell, Dez. Will you leave it.

DEZ. If Eileen could hear how you're speaking to me she'd be sick in her mouth.

I want to talk to her.

He goes to try and move to the bar, VALENTINE *blocks him.*

VALENTINE. You're not going upstairs.

DEZ. Charlene.

CHARLENE. What?

DEZ. Go and get her.

CHARLENE. I'm not getting her I can't just go and get her –

DEZ (*shouting up*). EILEEN!

VALENTINE. Dez –

DEZ. EILEEN?

VALENTINE. She can't hear you –

He tries again to get past.

DEZ. I need to talk to her.

VALENTINE. She's in Ireland.

DEZ. You left her in Ireland.

VALENTINE. She's still there.

DEZ. You left her on her own.

VALENTINE. She died actually.

DEZ. What?

Beat.

VALENTINE. Yeah she did she died on our second day.

CHARLENE. She can't have done –

VALENTINE. She did.

CHARLENE. You never said. I've been here and you've never said.

Beat.

VALENTINE. We buried her yesterday.

Beat.

DEZ. Is that true?

VALENTINE. Her sisters wanted to do it over there. They wanted to do it near her parents. The same plot.

Beat.

DEZ *leaves.*

CHARLENE. Are you okay?

VALENTINE. They let me brush her hair. She looked really nice. She'd have been pleased about that.

CHARLENE. Yeah.

VALENTINE. Wouldn't have wanted to be buried with all her hair sticking out here sort of thing.

CHARLENE. No you're right about that.

VALENTINE. We had fish and chips from the chipper on our first day. Sat and ate them together on the beach.

CHARLENE. That's really nice, Val.

VALENTINE. She got a fireman's lift from a Ryanair steward.

CHARLENE. I bet she loved that.

Beat.

VALENTINE. Will you sing something?

CHARLENE. There's nobody here.

VALENTINE. I want to listen to something.

CHARLENE *stands up, makes her way over to the microphone. She feels a bit awkward about this but she's about to sing. The intro to a song starts.* VALENTINE *is watching.* FRANKY *enters and pulls the plug out of the machine.*

FRANKY. Have you seen my dad?

CHARLENE. I thought you'd be eating sandwiches on the Avanti West Coast by now.

FRANKY. I'm not going back. I've decided.

CHARLENE. I was about to sing something.

FRANKY. I've had an argument with my dad.

CHARLENE. Valentine wanted me to sing.

FRANKY. I can't go back on an argument.

CHARLENE. I know what today is.

FRANKY. I feel like my head is gonna explode a bit.

Like someone's got their hands around my throat and my head is gonna burst open. That's what I feel like.

CHARLENE. Maybe you just need to let the dust settle.

FRANKY. I don't think I can stay at that house.

VALENTINE. You don't have to.

CHARLENE. You're lucky.

FRANKY. Am I?

CHARLENE. You've got somewhere else to go.

FRANKY. Do you remember when we talked about our flat.

CHARLENE. Yeah.

FRANKY. You wanted a bed with a desk underneath.

CHARLENE. Yeah well, I was fourteen when I said that.

FRANKY. Open-plan. Brand-new kitchen. We'd have a breakfast bar with a granite worktop.

You were obsessed with the granite worktop.

CHARLENE. They wipe down very easily.

FRANKY. We used to cut them out of brochures, Val. Flats on the Aimson Road.

VALENTINE. Did you?

FRANKY. If I stay, we could move into one.

CHARLENE. Who could.

FRANKY. Me and you. We could rent one of the flats on the Aimson Road.

CHARLENE. I can't.

FRANKY. I can make an appointment, we could go and look round one, it'll be like *Selling Sunset*.

CHARLENE. It won't.

FRANKY. I could start saving. I could put a little amount into a separate account and –

CHARLENE. I've been saving up for years.

FRANKY. Have you, Charl?

CHARLENE. I've been working since I was sixteen. I've got money in an ISA.

FRANKY. You never told me that you've been saving. You never mentioned –

CHARLENE. I got a promotion the other day.

FRANKY. I didn't know that.

CHARLENE. I've been promoted to assistant manager. I'll be in charge of the Baby Room.

FRANKY. That's –

CHARLENE. It's more money and I'll be good at it.

FRANKY. That's great cos you can put that money into your account and we can start looking. We can make a plan. We can look at flats on the High Road if the ones –

CHARLENE. I'm saving to buy a flat with Danny.

FRANKY. Who's Danny?

VALENTINE. Daniel Nicholson.

CHARLENE. He's my boyfriend.

FRANKY. What boyfriend?

CHARLENE. I haven't told you.

FRANKY. You haven't mentioned a boyfriend ever.

CHARLENE. I didn't want to.

FRANKY. He went to our primary school.

CHARLENE. We've been together for two-and-a-half years.

FRANKY. Why haven't you told me?

CHARLENE. Cos sometimes, Franky, it's like you're so scared
    of anyone's else joy not being yours that you have to take
    it and squash it or laugh at it or turn it into something that
    they're not very proud of any more.

FRANKY. Is that what you think?

CHARLENE. You've always got to be a little bit better than
    everyone else.

FRANKY. I don't feel like I am.

CHARLENE. When you left, you never even told me. You
    were like Jesy leaving Little Mix you got your mum to come
    round and tell me.

FRANKY. I didn't want to upset you.

CHARLENE. You thought I'd do nothing without you, Frank.

FRANKY. I've known you longer than I've known anyone else.

    Beat.

CHARLENE. We were never meant to be friends not really.

VALENTINE. Charl –

CHARLENE. My mum said she used to reward me with
    chocolate Penguins for every hour I played with you.

FRANKY. You were my first friend.

CHARLENE. I used to miss out on all the games with my sisters because I was playing with you.

I didn't understand any of their rules.

FRANKY. I used to hear you through the trees. I wanted to play with you because I could hear you through the trees.

CHARLENE. They used to ring the house phone non stop.

FRANKY. Who did.

CHARLENE. I realised I'd forgotten. The house phone ringing off the hook and Natalie sloping off upstairs in tears.

FRANKY. I don't know what you mean.

CHARLENE. Natalie was already on first fake ID and your mum and dad wanted her to come round and play with you.

FRANKY. No they didn't.

CHARLENE. So then they asked me.

FRANKY. They wouldn't do that. Why would they do that?

VALENTINE. They wanted it to be the same.

FRANKY. The same as what?

CHARLENE. They made me be your friend.

VALENTINE. You can't blame them for wanting it to be the same.

FRANKY. I feel like I don't know who I am. Like I've never really known. Not really.

CHARLENE. You can't fix him, Franky.

FRANKY. He isn't broke.

CHARLENE. You just need to talk to him.

FRANKY. I don't know where to find him.

CHARLENE. I do, Frank.

FRANKY. Do yer?

CHARLENE. I know where he'll be.

Scene Sixteen

Same night. Later. This is the Edge. It's a large stretch of moorland that rises above the town. On a clear day, you will see both Manchester and Liverpool. We can see that there is a pool of water, a reservoir, just below in the distance. DEZ, a lone figure, stares down into it. FRANKY enters from the path.

DEZ. I think it's amazing that view.

Do you think it's amazing?

FRANKY. I realised that in all the years I lived here I've never seen it before.

DEZ. That sound, Frank.

FRANKY. I can't hear anything.

DEZ. Exactly.

They listen to it.

Sometimes you might hear a bird hitting the water and the sound is just. It's unbelievable.

FRANKY. Used to say there was a creature in the water.

In school. That's what people used to say.

Used to say the creature would get you if you weren't careful. Some girls would come and smoke up here.

DEZ. You never fancied it.

FRANKY. You wouldn't let me.

DEZ. Smoke? No.

FRANKY. Come up here. I was never allowed.

DEZ. I was standing here once and a man came walking up with his bike. He put his bike to the side and he started going through that hole in the fence. I watched him going down towards the water. I knew as soon as I saw him what he was up to. Can you imagine? It's black that water.

FRANKY. Did he see you?

DEZ. I grabbed him. Held on to him like a fucking bear.
I pulled him down into the dirt. We sat there for ages.
He thanked me after, told me he would go home to bed and
then, and this is true, Frank, he walked over to his bike and
he took his helmet and he put it on top of his head and he
cycled off again. I thought… all that and you're putting your
helmet on. That bit of care for yourself, you know?

FRANKY. How did you do it? How did you stop him?

DEZ. Just talked to him. Just said something like –

'It won't stay like this.'

'It won't be like this every day.'

It's just that image sometimes. Him putting that helmet on,
fastening it under the chin. It could tear me in two.

I've never told anyone that before.

FRANKY. What if it is?

DEZ. What?

FRANKY. Every day. What if it does stay?

DEZ. I dunno. Is it not worth finding out?

Beat.

FRANKY. It was here wasn't it.

DEZ. You don't get summers like that any more.

FRANKY. I always thought she died in my bedroom.

DEZ. It's the guilt that eats you up.

FRANKY. Is it?

I've never really known anyone who's died.

DEZ. We went to see a doctor not long after it happened. Me
and your mum. That's what you do when someone, when
your child dies, the doctor you know what she told us to do?
She told us to go and find the nearest and the highest hill and
she said when you get to the top of it just let out a scream.
Imagine that. A doctor prescribing a scream. See how you
feel after that, she said. And when we left we just sat there

in silence in the car park and we never spoke about it again ever. I never went to see a doctor since.

FRANKY. Nobody's ever told me.

DEZ. I can't stop thinking about that scream, Frank. That maybe it would have helped.

FRANKY. Nobody's ever told me what happened.

DEZ. Too much water inside her lungs. They started to swell.

FRANKY. I think you and Mum thought I was just born knowing.

DEZ. It was a red-hot day. That's what I remember. She'd been climbing the walls all day. Temper tantrums, screaming abdabs. I said 'She needs fresh air, Lind, she's too hot in this house.'

I brought her here. That's what people did back then. They came here, to the reservoir, to cool off. We took a little picnic. It was just a packet of crisps, sandwiches in tin foil, but we called it Our Picnic. Everyone was there. Valentine and his mates. Her friend, Natalie, and her mum. She liked the water. She liked swimming. We used to call her Our Little Fish.

One minute she was licking the salt off the inside of a crisp packet and the next she's in the water, swimming across to her friend and then in absolutely no time at all, in the light of the same day, with the earth still turning underneath you, you find yourself in the middle of a hospital corridor with no socks and shoes on and a doctor is standing in front of you telling you –

that's it.

That's when you feel like running through the wall.

FRANKY You called me by her name once.

DEZ. I didn't mean to –

FRANKY. I came home for the weekend with Alfie and you, you were making fried eggs in the pan. You asked me to pass you the salt from the side and you called me her name. Pass that would you, and you said her name –

That's what you said.

DEZ. It was an accident.

FRANKY. And it scared me actually –

DEZ. Did it?

FRANKY. Cos I was twenty-two wasn't I? I was twenty-two when you said that and she, well she was only seven when she died.

DEZ. Yeah.

FRANKY. It was before I was born.

And they don't even have the same letters. They don't sound similar at all.

Franky and Grace.

DEZ. No they don't.

FRANKY. I knew then that it was right at the front. That it always had been.

DEZ. You missed my sixtieth.

FRANKY. What?

DEZ. You missed my sixtieth birthday.

FRANKY. I told you there was rail replacements –

DEZ. It was only three weeks after and you missed it.

FRANKY. It would have taken me six hours on a bus.

DEZ. You didn't want to come.

FRANKY. It confused me.

DEZ. It was an accident.

Beat.

FRANKY. There's all her things in my room.

DEZ. I know.

FRANKY. And I was thinking if you and Mum ever die what will I do with all that stuff. There will be so much stuff.

DEZ. You don't need to worry about any of that.

FRANKY. I feel like I do. There's nobody else. Who will go to her grave? Who will look after it?

DEZ. I don't know.

FRANKY. I don't think I can make people feel happy.

DEZ. That's never true. It couldn't be possible.

FRANKY. Sometimes it feels like all your happy memories are before me.

DEZ. Is that what you think?

FRANKY. It's meant to mean something isn't it. My life. It has to mean something.

DEZ. Doesn't everyone's?

FRANKY. I was meant to put you back together. But I can't. And sometimes I feel like I need putting back together too.

You're looking at me funny.

DEZ. You know you were just an idea in the middle of the night once. A could we, would we, should we dare to do that again?

Look at you now.

FRANKY. I'm nearly twenty-four.

I've not really done anything out of the ordinary, Dad.

DEZ. You've got your job. You're good at it.

FRANKY. It's just a job. It doesn't fill me up.

DEZ. You're good at it.

FRANKY. What if I'm just this. Right in front of you.

DEZ. You're alive, Frank.

Have I ever told you about the night you were born?

FRANKY. No.

DEZ. Seven forty-six on the fifteenth of September.

I ran all the way from the hospital to the pub just to tell everyone. Eileen poured champagne into flutes.

I ran three miles in jeans.

As FRANKY *listens to this she moves ever so slightly away from* DEZ.

FRANKY. Dad –

DEZ. I'm sorry about your rabbit.

FRANKY. It's okay.

DEZ. It's not okay. I shouldn't have –

FRANKY. He was the best one.

DEZ. Well there's only one Paul Scholes, Frank.

FRANKY. That was Paul Scholes the third. We replaced him twice.

Me and my mum used to go to Pets at Home when you were at work.

DEZ. You pair of bastards.

The whole point of getting you the thing was so you – ah forget it.

FRANKY. Did you really think a rabbit could live for sixteen years?

They both really laugh at this and then a silence falls.

DEZ. Are you okay, Franky?

FRANKY. Sometimes I am.

DEZ. But not always.

FRANKY. I don't know if I am.

DEZ. I wish you were.

FRANKY. I know.

FRANKY *moves towards the water.*

DEZ. I wish you could be. What are you doing?

She ignores him and is so close to the water that her feet might be in it now.

You're not supposed to do that. You'll get your feet wet.

FRANKY. It's fine look.

She moves into the water, fully.

DEZ. Don't, Frank, please –

FRANKY. I'm okay.

Here.

He stands up.

DEZ. What?

FRANKY. It's warm a bit.

DEZ. Is it?

DEZ *staggers down towards her.*

FRANKY. It is yeah.

It's had the sun on it all day.

DEZ *walks right to the the edge of the water. His feet
might get wet and we feel as though he might go in further.
A moment of total quiet and stillness.*

Scene Seventeen

*A few days later. Light pours down on The Sun Inn. DEZ is
inspecting damage to the floor.*

VALENTINE *walks in.*

DEZ. There's water underneath your floorboards.

VALENTINE. You're early.

DEZ. Door was open, Val.

VALENTINE. The wood has rotted. It's gone soft.

I started trying to pull it up. I think I've made it worse.

DEZ. It can't stay like that. It needs to be replaced.

VALENTINE. The whole thing?

DEZ. It needs ripping right out. I'll help you to rip it right out.

VALENTINE. It's not a small job, Dez.

DEZ. I'll bring my tools.

VALENTINE. When?

DEZ. Tomorrow. We can do it together.

VALENTINE. Right. Well. Thanks –

> DEZ *continues looking at it. He's looking at how he could do the job.* VALENTINE *brings tumblers down from the bar. He fills them with whiskey.* CHARLENE *enters in her silver puffa jacket.*

CHARLENE. Where is everyone?

VALENTINE. Not here yet.

CHARLENE. Well I can't stay for long I've got my first day as assistant manager tomorrow.

VALENTINE. Have you?

CHARLENE. Can't turn up as assistant manager stinking of drink.

> LINDA *and* FRANKY *enter together.*

LINDA. It's a lovely day outside. Did anyone notice?

VALENTINE. I've not been out yet.

FRANKY. We've been for a walk in the sunshine.

CHARLENE. Have you?

LINDA. Big blue sky.

You want to see it.

DEZ. I've got two kilos of lamb mince in the fridge.

FRANKY. What?

DEZ. I went to the butcher's.

FRANKY. When?

DEZ. This morning.

I thought –

What about a barbecue?

FRANKY. A barbecue.

DEZ. This afternoon.

FRANKY. I've got a train at twenty past seven.

CHARLENE. Have you?

FRANKY. Yeah. I've booked it. I'm going back.

DEZ. We can do it before you leave.

FRANKY. Will you come round, Mum?

LINDA. I could do some Sangria if you want. I'll have to get some Fanta from the shop.

DEZ. I've got some. I bought a bottle this morning.

Do you like lamb, Val?

VALENTINE. Yeah I like lamb.

DEZ. Have you ever tried my lamb kebabs?

VALENTINE. I don't think I have.

DEZ. What about my yogurt sauce?

VALENTINE. No I've never tried it.

DEZ. Charlene?

CHARLENE. What?

DEZ. Do you want to come?

CHARLENE. I don't know.

FRANKY. You could bring Daniel if you want.

CHARLENE. I'll think about it.

Beat.

I'm glad you're going back, Frank. I'm happy for you.

FRANKY. Thanks.

VALENTINE. I quit my job.

FRANKY. Did you?

VALENTINE. Yeah. Yesterday. I just walked in and I quit.

DEZ. You're our new landlord.

VALENTINE. Yeah. Well. Sort of.

FRANKY. Not sort of.

LINDA. You *are*.

VALENTINE. Yeah I suppose.

DEZ. It's in your bones, Val.

CHARLENE. Val.

VALENTINE. What?

CHARLENE. Them drinks will go stagnant if you leave them any longer.

VALENTINE. Whiskey doesn't spoil, Charl.

VALENTINE *hands around the drinks.*

FRANKY. Go on then.

Silence.

CHARLENE. Did you not write anything down?

Silence.

VALENTINE. Right well –

Silence.

LINDA. I was thinking last night about how Eileen would take having a good time very seriously.

VALENTINE. Yeah she would.

LINDA. How she couldn't stand it if other people weren't having a good time.

How she would cut her own arm off if it would mean making one of us laugh. She always seemed to know when something was bothering one of us. She'd bring us inside, play some music and fix us a drink.

And then she'd never speak about it ever again.

She made us feel better.

VALENTINE. Thanks Lind.

DEZ *raises his glass.*

DEZ. A toast?

VALENTINE. Yeah.

They raise their glasses.

DEZ. To *Your Nana* and to *Our Friend.* And –

to all the ones who live in here.

He touches his chest. They cheers, clink glasses, drink.

FRANKY. I got you this.

FRANKY *unwraps a framed newspaper article. There's a picture there of Eileen smiling.*

VALENTINE *reads it aloud.*

VALENTINE. The oldest landlady in the country.

FRANKY. She made it.

LINDA. Are you okay?

VALENTINE. Yeah I am. I feel really happy.

DEZ. It's absolutely fantastic that.

LINDA. You should put it up behind the bar.

They all watch as he does this. Silence.

DEZ. Will you be wanting a lift to the station later?

FRANKY. I can order a taxi, Dad.

DEZ. I'll give you a lift.

FRANKY. You don't have to.

DEZ. I'd like to give you a lift.

FRANKY. Okay.

DEZ. I'll drive you to the station and drop you off by the Tesco Express.

FRANKY. After the barbecue?

DEZ. Yeah after that.

FRANKY. Okay then yeah.

VALENTINE. I think I will put some music on.

LINDA. If you want to.

VALENTINE. I could switch the machine on. What if I did that? If I switched the machine on.

Someone could sing if they want?

VALENTINE *goes over to the karaoke machine, he switches it on and it starts to come to life. As he does this,* DEZ *starts singing. It's 'Peggy Gordon'. This is something he hasn't sang in years and years. It's for Eileen and it comes straight from his chest.*

Lights out.

'The Whole of the Moon' by The Waterboys plays.

End.

A Nick Hern Book

Heart Wall first published in Great Britain in 2026 as a paperback original by Nick Hern Books Limited, The Glasshouse, 49a Goldhawk Road, London W12 8QP, in association with the Bush Theatre, London

Heart Wall copyright © 2026 Kit Withington

Kit Withington has asserted her right to be identified as the author of this work.

Cover photograph by Isaac Marley Morgan

Designed and typeset by Nick Hern Books, London
Printed in the UK by Mimeo Ltd, Huntingdon, Cambridgeshire PE29 6XX

A CIP catalogue record for this book is available from the British Library

ISBN 978 1 83904 551 6

www.nickhernbooks.co.uk/environmental-policy

Nick Hern Books' authorised representative in the EU is
Easy Access System Europe – Mustamäe tee 50, 10621 Tallinn, Estonia
email gpsr.requests@easproject.com